Living Lutheran

Other books in the Lutheran Voices series

See www.lutheranvoices.com

Living Lutheran
Renewing Your Congregation

Dave Daubert

Augsburg Fortress

Minneapolis

Dedicated to my wife, Marlene,
and our children, Erin and Nathan

LIVING LUTHERAN
Renewing Your Congregation

Large-quantity purchases or custom editions of these books are available at a discount from the publisher. For more information, contact the sales department at Augsburg Fortress, Publishers, 1-800-328-4648, or write to: Sales Director, Augsburg Fortress, Publishers, P.O. Box 1209, Minneapolis, MN 55440-1209.

Scripture quotations are from the *New Revised Standard Version Bible*, copyright © 1989 by the Division of Christian Education of the National Council of the Churches of Christ in the U.S.A. Used by permission. All rights reserved.

Pages 26, 34, and 79 contain portions of *The Small Catechism* by Martin Luther (Minneapolis: Augsburg Fortress, 1979). Used by permission.

Library of Congress Cataloging-in-Publication Data
Daubert, Dave, 1960-
  Living Lutheran : renewing your congregation / by Dave Daubert.
      p. cm.— (Lutheran voices)
  Includes bibliographical references.
  ISBN-10: 0-8066-5334-5 (pbk. : alk. paper), ISBN-13: 978-0-8066-5334-1
  1. Lutheran Church. 2. Church renewal. I. Title.
  BX8018.D38 2007
  284.1—dc22   2006034005

Editor: Susan Johnson
Cover Design: © Koechel Peterson and Associates, Inc., Minneapolis, MN
          www.koechelpeterson.com; Cover photo © Design Pics/Punchstock

The paper used in this publication meets the minimum requirements of American National Standard for Information Sciences—Permanence of Paper for Printed Library Materials, ANSI Z329.48-1984.

Manufactured in the U.S.A.

11   10   09   08   4   5   6   7   8   9   10

Contents

Preface

Although I didn't know it until I was an adult, my Christian journey began as an infant. Having been blessed with good parents, good siblings, and good friends, I grew up knowing I was valuable and loved. Even many in the church struggle to find that security. Although I was essentially unchurched, I was baptized as a baby by my great-grandfather who was a pastor in the Presbyterian church. My parents brought me to Sunday school for a while in elementary school. My best friend Tom was an active Christian and we talked often about matters of God. Mr. Frisina, my science teacher and also a Methodist minister on weekends, encouraged me to ask questions and keep God in the mix. These people shaped me in many ways. I am grateful to all of them.

But I became more conscious of my Christian journey because two friends, Scott and John, dared to invite me to church while I was at Virginia Tech. When I said no to their invitation they filtered it and heard "not yet." So they asked me again and again, never pushing but always inviting. When I finally went to church with them, I began to see a community of people committed to what God was up to. I found Jesus to be more than a figure from history. He was a living Savior who brought new life with his presence.

I met my wife Marlene in the Lutheran church. We were both active and involved. But when she gave me a Bible for a wedding present, it caught me by surprise and made me think. (I gave her a cruise control—it was what she asked for!) A few months later I told her I was leaving engineering to go to seminary. (She cried.) Twenty years later she went to seminary. (God has a sense of humor!) Today she is a diaconal minister in our church and a great partner for ministry, and I am blessed to spend my life's journey with her.

At seminary I was blessed by many fine and faithful people, three whose influence finds its way into this book. Walter Bouman, Walter Taylor, and Wayne Stumme all taught me about theology, scripture, and mission in ways too numerous to detail here. While working with Wayne, my thesis adviser, I first really dug into the book of Acts. The readings at the end of each chapter in this book come from the Acts of the Apostles because it is such a great place to see a missional church in action.

I have been blessed to be pastor of two congregations—Hilltop Lutheran Church in Columbus, Ohio, and Zion Lutheran Church in Elgin, Illinois—and I have learned most of what is in this book through working with the great laity who comprise the core and frontline of the church. When we all recognize that truth, the church will be changed! To the people of St. Matthew Lutheran Church in Omaha, Nebraska, and Bethel Lutheran Church in Palatine, Illinois, I am thankful for the church home that you provided for my family and me. I have been blessed to work with Bishop Richard Jessen and his staff in Nebraska, which allowed me to see congregational life from the outside in. (Things do look different from different perspectives!) The same has been true working with Pastor Richard Magnus and the staff of what is now the unit for Evangelical Outreach and Congregational Mission in Chicago.

As a part of my work in the churchwide organization I help oversee transformation of congregations. Although most of this book was developed in congregational ministry, it was articulated and shaped in partnership with a team of great people who have taught me much about their own experiences in congregational life. The team includes Kelly Fryer, Helen Harms, Steve Kanouse, Tana Kjos, and Beth Yenchko. I am indebted to them for their friendship, partnership, and all they bring to the work of renewal.

Lastly, I need to mention my two children, Erin (a senior in high school as I write this) and Nathan (a high school freshman). In the adventure that is parenting, Marlene and I have been blessed to receive them as gift. As Nila, a member of our congregation, reminds all parents, "They aren't yours. God loans them to you for a little while." I was unchurched at their age. While Erin and Nathan are both deeply involved in the life of the church, they also represent much that is typical of people in their generation, most of whom are not involved in the church. Their peers are the most unchurched generation in American history. They often remind me that much about church life seems boring and irrelevant to them, and they are right. If millions of people are going to meet Jesus and discover in him the face of a God who loves them, our churches are going to have to change and get back out in the world making a difference. Getting back to the core of the church is going to be essential. In the end, that's why this book was written.

A final note: All who read this book will be better prepared and blessed to read the entire book of Acts before they dig in here. Most people can read it easily in less than two hours. What follows will make more sense if you do!

1

A Changing Church for a Changing World

I grew up in a small town in upstate New York. We had five churches in town. All were Christian. The largest was the Roman Catholic church to which about sixty percent of the town belonged. The Protestants were covered by the Baptist church, the Episcopal church, the Presbyterian church, and the United Methodist church. Although my family didn't go to church, we were still semi-affiliated with the Methodists. My parents essentially thought church was irrelevant, but there was enough cultural pressure that during my elementary years they dropped me off at Sunday school, at least until I asked to not go any more because it was boring.

In that world, even though my parents thought church was of marginal value, I still had a connection to the church. My parents felt some obligation to get me a basic Christian foundation so I would know good from evil and right from wrong. It was assumed to be the right thing to do even if you didn't buy into the whole package. The church held a central function in the culture of the day. As the church, we taught people to be good citizens, and the world sent us people and kept us going.

I call this model "the church at the center." In any culture there are various things at the core. In the 1950s as the Cold War was at its height, godless communism vs. a Godly America was a primary paradigm for us to interpret life. Christianity, especially Protestant Christianity, was a mark of being a loyal American. In 1954 the Pledge of Allegiance was changed to include the words "under God." During a recent discussion about whether or not the

American flag should be displayed in the sanctuary, I learned 1954 was the same year the Boy Scouts began to give out merit badges for "God and Country." Within that worldview, church was one of the things at the core of culture.

In many ways the church was at its apex—enjoying the power of being respected and needed. In this kind of a "you scratch my back and I'll scratch yours" world the church blessed the culture with a sense of Godliness and righteousness. In return, the culture sent people in record numbers to attend and support the church. Even if parents didn't attend church, they brought their children to Sunday school because it was the right thing to do. Even children raised by agnostic parents probably had a devout relative or two (in my case I also had an especially devout set of great-grandparents). Almost no one would consider not bringing a child to church to be baptized. Being a Christian was seen as the norm. "Normal" people went to church. You can look at the diagram below to see a graphic of how this might look.

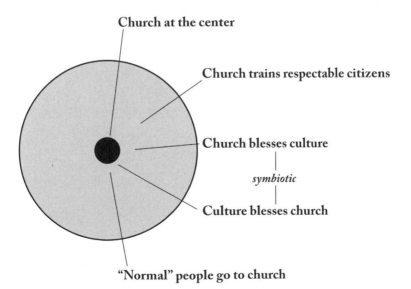

Church at the center

Church trains respectable citizens

Church blesses culture

symbiotic

Culture blesses church

"Normal" people go to church

Today things have changed. There are no drop-off kids in the congregation where I now serve. Not one! We have a few kids connecting with the ministry of our congregation in some way who come to Sunday school on their own. But their parents don't bring them or even care very much whether or not they go. Parents raised as unchurched children in the 1970s and 1980s may not have any idea what's going on in our church buildings. This means that our Sunday schools are generally much smaller than they used to be. Children and adults who come to church today are more likely to do so because it matters in some way in their lives and not because popular culture says it is the proper thing to do. In fact, there's little in today's culture to even suggest that good people go to church and Sunday school.

These changes began in earnest during the 1960s. The end of the baby boom coincided with the civil rights movement, the Vietnam crisis, and the Watergate scandal. Those events precipitated the integration of what had been isolated, homogenous communities. Traditional values were challenged by a willingness to entertain diverse ideas. Public trust in authority diminished, causing people to question institutions, including the church. A church at the center of society seemed to some to be complicit with the dominant culture and as likely to support the bad guys as the good ones. Some began to think that maybe church wasn't a place to learn good values after all. Maybe it was just one more boring, irrelevant thing to do to preserve the status quo. Church membership and attendance began to decline. From the 1970s on, the church that had been mainline in the 1950s and 1960s has steadily moved toward the margins of society.

Many people, including me, think that the number of people who attend church in a typical week may be as few as one in five U.S. residents. In the Pacific Northwest the number one religious preference from the census data was "none." That means that more people have no religious affiliation than are connected with any other single religious group. This has never before been the case in the United States. While there are regional variations in participation, no region of the United States can confidently say that even half of its residents attend worship regularly. What was once a centrist activity and assumed to be part of respectable people's lives is now a fringe activity in many places.

Inside the Evangelical Lutheran Church in America the picture is similar. In 2005 our membership roles dropped to below five million members for the first time. Across the country less than one third of those people are in church on Sunday. Average weekly worship attendance is only about one and a half million people. In general, these numbers have shown a slow but steady decline for decades.

The church that once lived at the center of culture and thrived as a result is now being moved more and more to the edges, maybe even the margins of society. It is now abnormal to go to church. If only one in five people are in church, attending worship is now a minority activity. In one town within the school district where I currently live, a church was challenged as they tried to get zoning approved to build a church building. The church lost. The town would rather have some other business there that pays taxes. The church is no longer seen as an asset but a liability.

From within the church, often the world gets blamed for changing. I will hear something like, "We were once really thriving here. We had a big Sunday school with lots of kids. The pews were filled almost every Sunday. Yeah, this was some church back then." When I ask what happened, in almost every case the response is something like, "The neighborhood changed. Our people moved to other neighborhoods. They would keep driving in for a while, but ultimately they'd find a church in their new neighborhood. And the new people in our neighborhood weren't like us. The new people just weren't Lutherans and they didn't really fit in here. We were fine until the neighborhood changed."

As attending a church becomes a minority activity and as the world pays less and less attention to what we have to say, the picture of the church at the center is changed. The church finds itself out somewhere closer to the edge of society. See the diagram below for a picture of how this might look today.

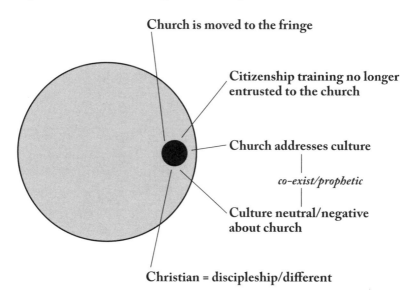

Church is moved to the fringe

Citizenship training no longer entrusted to the church

Church addresses culture

co-exist/prophetic

Culture neutral/negative about church

Christian = discipleship/different

Some Christians see the church being pushed from the center out to the margins. Some groups may even protest or try to legislate in ways to protect the church's role and power. But I see the world as changing and the church as having stood still too long. We have not been pushed to the side. We have taken our role as the church for granted for so long that the world has changed and passed us by. We have not been pushed to the margins. We have pretended that we could stand still and keep up with God and the world. We now find out that we can't. A changing world demands a changing church.

One response to numbers like these is for the church to become interested in evangelism. During the 1990s the ELCA had a churchwide evangelism strategy. In 2000, as that strategy was being evaluated, we discovered that in spite of all the good work we had done, the church had continued to shrink. Thousands of hours and millions of dollars were spent on evangelism and yet both membership and worship attendance had declined. To find out why this happened, the ELCA Department for Research and Evaluation did a study of all the evangelism work that was done.[1] The study showed that in spite of the fact that the ELCA as a whole had shrunk, within our churches there were still some vibrant, relevant, and growing ministries.

What was the difference between these vibrant ministries and the more typical Lutheran congregation? The study showed that declining and growing congregations were doing the same things. Getting a better sign, adding a contemporary worship service, putting ads in the paper showed up in both fast growing and fast shrinking ministries.

While similar techniques and tactics were applied by both groups of churches, the congregations that were vibrant and growing and had a real impact were almost always clear about two things. First, they were clear about their purpose or their vision for ministry. They had an understanding of what God was doing and how they could be a part of that. It was known and shared by the membership. It was as important to many in the pews as it was to the pastors in the pulpit. Second, these vibrant congregations showed an openness to change in order to be faithful. "We've never done it that way before," was replaced with, "What do we need to do to be effective for God?"

On the other hand, struggling congregations were focused most often on their own survival and not much else. When asked about God's purpose for their ministry, they lacked clarity and commitment to mission. There was no purpose. Vision was dim. In addition, these places reported little enthusiasm for change. They would try something if it would keep them alive, but it didn't bring a sense of wonder and adventure. It was received as a burden.

In short, evangelism simply to recruit members for the church doesn't work. God isn't interested in a bigger church as much as God is interested in a transformed world. Renewing ministry means reconnecting the church with what God is up to in the world. A renewed congregation exists for others more than for itself. It sees partnering with God as exciting and adventuresome—a chance to extend God's love to others and to meet new people who will be allies in God's work.

The study also showed that the only logical place for the church to begin to implement transformation is with those of us who love the church and are already followers of Jesus. We start with us because we are the only people we can change. If we are not clear about our purpose, clear about what is important and open to being changed by God, then nothing else is likely to happen. And if we are not serious about this new life that comes from Christ, why would we expect someone else to be? Sadly, too many Lutherans have been lulled into believing, "If we could just get some new people in here, this church would really do something." Why would we trust that people we have not yet met will be more committed to this than we are? The task of becoming better disciples starts one life at a time, and the process begins with us.

With this in mind, we now turn to the start of our work. To engage a world with the gospel means that no longer can we just say the religious words that popular culture has expected us to speak. The words have become such platitudes that they have long lost their sense of power. People have stopped listening to us. We aren't sure really what difference it makes to be a Christian, even in our own lives. Our first task is to reclaim a voice that is uniquely ours and has something to say to a world that is hungry for a word of life that can come only from God. If the church is to renew, we have to find our own Lutheran voices for the twenty-first century.

2

The Basics of a Lutheran Voice

The work of renewing a congregation is not an easy task. The odds are against you. In some places the church is still functional enough that it can live in denial a little longer, but it shouldn't! Old, familiar voices speak quietly in our heads, reminding us of a heyday when the church was bigger and seemed so much more important than it does now. Often these old voices are not our best Lutheran voice. They are ghosts from our past. They may have served us well once, but they no longer can be the voice we hear loudest or the voice with which we speak. To be a new church we need to listen to a new voice and bring a new word to the church and to the world in which we live.

Renewing a congregation, truly bringing about transformation, means putting your best efforts forward. This means your best thinking. It means your best actions. It means devoting your best resources to the work. Very few declining congregations change. It is too comfortable and easy to stay the way they are. So if you are reading this book hoping to find new life for your congregation, the first word to you is that it is likely to be tough.

That word isn't shared with you to discourage you. In fact, it is to encourage you to take stock of the journey ahead for you and for others who are part of your congregation. You can't do this alone. Changing a congregation is a communal task—no one of us is church by ourselves. So as you are reading this book, the first word of encouragement is for you to find a friend or group of friends to read it with you. The work inside this book will be a mix of hard work and fun, but when done in partnership with others, it all can be rewarding.

A key to the process is that someone needs to start it. Congregations do not change by themselves. Nor do they change collectively. In the process of change, some people will be ahead while others may never be on board. Those who are ahead and have a vision or are hungering to find a vision need to take the lead. No congregation will transform if leadership is not present and willing to press the issue. This is nothing new. The Bible basically is a series of stories that tell how God called people to do various things at which they either succeeded or failed. God works through people. God calls some forth to be leaders.

This book's philosophy of leadership is grounded in people who are able to engage others. There is no assumption that the leader will know all the answers. Rather, the leaders in this process will be the ones who sense that God is saying something to the congregation about its ministry. They are willing to push for the people to listen to God in a new way. That means that a leader may not see where the community is going any better than anyone else. But the leader believes that the community is called to go somewhere and is willing to risk raising the question and calling forth people to pray with him or her, to study scripture together, and to begin a discussion to try to clarify what God is saying to the church and what the congregation is going to do about it. This is not about leaders who provide easy answers. It is about leaders with the courage to ask the hard questions and to engage God in order to find the answers. Leaders in this model are called on to get people thinking and talking

Purposeful discussion is not optional work for the church. The thesis for my doctor of ministry degree in preaching dealt with the use of discussion groups after sermons. In a class lecture I had heard Walter Brueggemann say, "It starts with utterance which invokes real conversations among the faithful and that leads to mission."[2] This is a major paradigm shift when you think about how much church communication is based primarily on hearing. The pastor preaches and the people listen. Brueggemann's middle step of "real conversations among the faithful" is often nowhere to be found. My goal was to see if people who talked about sermons would be more missional. Was Brueggemann right?

What I discovered shocked me. I preached sermons at congregations one Sunday and then surveyed the same congregations a week later. Of the people who had not talked about the sermon only nine percent could even remember the topic of the message well enough to suggest anything about how it might apply to the church's mission. But among those who talked about the sermon, almost eighty-five percent had suggestions for applying the theme of the sermon to the church's mission.

What was fascinating was that it didn't matter whether they were in some organized group or if they reported talking about it in the car with family members on the way home from church. If they remembered a significant conversation about the sermon, they remembered the sermon. What I realized was that it wasn't the sermon they remembered—it was the conversation! And if they remembered the sermon because they talked about it, then they had a suggestion on how the congregation could apply it—something to consider doing as a result.

Most of us learn more in community that we do by ourselves. Almost all of us learn more when we discuss what we have listened to or read than when we simply listen to someone else or read their words on a page. The act of speaking requires us to put thoughts together, to synthesize ideas and turn them into points that other people recognize when they hear them. In short, when we speak as a student, we begin to switch roles and become the teacher. The smartest people don't just learn a lot, they teach. Oddly enough, the act of teaching helps the teacher integrate the material and makes both the students and the teacher smarter. Long term, teachers get as much out of their classes as most of their students. So find companions for the journey to discuss what God is up to, and each of you will have moments to share ideas and teach others.

This book is a part of the Lutheran Voices series. The goal of this book is to help you discover your own "Lutheran voice." The questions and exercises at the end of each chapter are there to help you say what is most important about being a Lutheran in the context in which you find yourself. This may be something you can read alone but it is not a journey you can take alone. This book is to help congregations work together to define what is most important about being in mission where you are.

The series title Lutheran Voices is broader than we might first realize. It is significant because the word *voices* is plural. The series is a place to lift up many voices within the Lutheran tradition. There is not just one voice that makes up the Evangelical Lutheran Church in America. Some strands of Lutheranism are very doctrinal. Within those strands, there is always a Lutheran answer (a Lutheran voice in the singular if you will). That voice tells the Lutheran position on whatever issue is to be addressed. For people who think this way, Lutheranism is about a theological system, laid out first in the Augsburg Confession and formulated in a permanent and almost final form in the *Book of Concord*. We need only know the Lutheran answer to the question, perhaps apply it to the current specific issue or question facing us, and a Lutheran stance will clearly emerge.

I have a deep respect for the Lutheran confessions. I refer to them often in my ministry. I love the energy that went into them and the commitment to faithfulness in which the confessions are grounded. But I don't think that they give us the last word on what constitutes a Lutheran voice. They are a foundational word that helps us to see through a certain lens what God is doing. They shape a worldview and help us frame our thoughts and conversations in a word that is grounded in scripture, indebted to Luther's struggles and insights, and continues on a conversation and articulation of what God has done and continues to do through Jesus Christ. It is fresh and new and calls for each of us to add our voice to the conversation and ultimately the proclamation of the gospel for today.

This book is designed to help you find your Lutheran voice and add it to the mix. It will ask you to do this in partnership with others so that the congregation where you serve will be a clearer Lutheran voice in the community where God has sent you to work. The goal is that all of us will lift our Lutheran voices more boldly together to be a better Lutheran witness and presence in the culture in which we find ourselves today.

The three keys to finding our Lutheran voice for our work together will be Bible study, prayer, and dialog. Each of these provides an essential part of coming together and finding a Lutheran voice.

The first key to finding our Lutheran voice is the practice of reading scripture. The Reformation relied heavily on the scriptures for all foundational changes. The term *Sola scriptura* (word alone) acknowledges that we understand God already has done and said much to engage the world with the gospel and that the record of God's activity in scripture is an essential foundation for the work of the church. In the ELCA we see scripture as the "source and norm" of our Christian faith. Reading scripture shapes our faith and helps our eyes to see and our ears to hear what God continues to say and do in our world today. How would we recognize God's voice or actions without some idea of where to look and what to look for? The scriptures give us this lens. They help us understand that to which God is committed and help us see what God is doing.

The discipline of prayer is essential because the focus of prayer connects us with a living God. Lutherans have always started with God. God acts and we respond. It should be no surprise that to find a Lutheran voice will mean finding a voice that is grounded in what God is saying to us. This means that we cannot simply speak to God when we pray. Finding a Lutheran voice will mean that we may have to learn to listen better to what God is saying during times of prayer. A healthy prayer life will lift up issues and struggles to God and then provide for time to listen and reflect on what God is saying. This means learning to make space for silence and learning to use it well. It may take different forms for different people. Many people set up a place where they can sit quietly to listen to what God is saying. As someone who doesn't sit still well, this method doesn't work for me. I need to go for a walk, wander through a labyrinth, or use the long amount of time that I spend commuting for listening. The key is to find a way to pray deeply and to listen and reflect on what God is saying to you in prayer. A Lutheran voice can only be Lutheran if it is clearly connected to what God is saying.

A third part of finding our Lutheran voice is dialog—the "real conversations of the faithful" that Walter Brueggemann called forth from us. Lutherans always have had a high regard for the church. As the assembly of believers, it is formed by a faith that gathers the faithful. It is not a separate thing apart from people. It is made up of the people whom Christ has claimed and made his own. The role of dialog in finding a Lutheran voice is then essential. In his work, *Life Together,* Dietrich Bonhoeffer wrote, "The mark of solitude is silence, just as speech is the mark of community" (*Dietrich Bonhoeffer Works,* Volume 5 [Minneapolis: Fortress Press], p. 83).

Because it is filled with people who make up the priesthood of all believers, the church is filled with people who can listen to God and approach God. In fact, each Christian is charged with the task of regularly speaking to God on behalf of others and speaking to others on behalf of God. Lutherans believe that each of us has something to contribute as we articulate God's word in and to our world. It is only through speaking and listening to each other that we can discern what God is saying to all of us as the church. Dialog is essential in order to truly be the church.

What does this look like in a vibrant congregation? Church becomes a place where people of faith gather to engage one another. They pray together. They read scripture together. They spend time in conversation—checking in with each other about how God has used them through the week, helping each other discern what God is calling forth from them in the coming week, and centering the community of faith on what God is calling forth from the church in that place. Such congregations may still talk about the weather and sports and they may still serve coffee and donuts. But their fellowship will be more intentional about including conversations where they see God in action. And they will be sure that they spend time listening to God speak to them. A vibrant and renewing congregation regards God's voice as the center of the community and treasures each person's voice as it reflects the voice of God into their midst.

So this Lutheran Voices book will be a little different than some others in the series. If it is effective it will result in a lot of Lutheran voices rather than articulating only one. Each chapter will encourage engagement with certain aspects of renewal from a Lutheran perspective. Then each chapter will conclude with questions or exercises that are grounded in scripture study, prayer, and dialogue. The work that you do in your place will bring the possibility of a clearer Lutheran voice where you live. If your heart is open to encounter a living God, if your ears can listen respectfully to others, and if you are able to share words about what you hear and see God doing (both in scripture and today), then you are ready for this process to begin. Let's get started.

For Reflection and Discussion

Remember that while these readings and exercises can be done alone, they are best done with others in a small-group setting. The experience of community Bible study and prayer and the importance of conversations are essential parts of the work of transforming the church and finding your Lutheran voices.

Read Acts 2:41-47. What you do see as standing at the center of early Christian life?

Pray, *God of the Word, we know that you have spoken in many and various ways through the prophets of old. But now you speak to us in these last days through the Word made flesh in Jesus. The voice of Christ has come to us in scripture and through the words of others and often we have been too busy to hear. Speak to us now. Help us to listen.*

Pause for a time of silence and listen for God's answer. Then close with the Lord's Prayer, pausing after "your kingdom come, your will be done on earth as in heaven." Repeat that part of the prayer and then continue through to the end.

Discuss the following:
1. When you gather on Sunday morning, what do most people talk about? How many people in your congregation would you estimate had a significant conversation with another member about what Jesus was doing in their lives during the week?

2. How many people in your congregation meet regularly with others to read scripture and talk about what they understand God to be saying or doing? Do you think this needs to change? If so, how might you get more people reading and discussing scripture?

3. How often do you pray with others in your congregation? Do most people assume that others are praying for them or is there a culture that intentionally fosters prayer with people as they are together?

4. At a typical committee meeting of your congregation, how much time is spent on (a) just chit-chat; (b) Bible study and prayer; and (c) getting down to business? How might this need to change in order to hear better God's voice and to work based on God's call?

3

God Has a Dream

I have mixed feelings about a lot of contemporary Christian music. While some songs are great, original stuff, other songs seem as if they were composed from a cookie cutter formula. I just can't handle it.

One Christian musician I do enjoy is Peter Mayer. He and his brother Jim grew up in India, sons of a Lutheran missionary couple. The experience of growing up in such a unique setting has given the Mayer brothers a special insight into the church that many of us in this country miss. In addition, Jim and Peter have been musicians in Jimmy Buffet's band for many years. When they are not playing Christian music they are mixing it up in huge stadiums and outdoor venues playing fun songs for all the "parrotheads" who flock to their shows.

One of my favorite songs that Peter sings is called, "God Is Loose in the World." It brings energy and a helpful reminder to those of us who spend too much time inside the church: God is out there! If you want to see what God is up to, then you have to look at more than the inside of a church building. You have to look out there! God is active twenty-four/seven! Even when church buildings are empty and the lights are off, God is busy out in the world doing all sorts of things.

The fact that God does more than show up for communion on Sunday mornings is obvious to anyone who has a vibrant faith. Most people know God is doing all sorts of things. Luther's explanation of the First Article of the Apostle's Creed reminds us of God's action in our lives.

God has created me together with all living creatures. God has given me and still preserves my body and soul. . . . God daily and abundantly provides. . . . God protects me against all danger and shields and preserves me from all evil. God does all this out of pure, fatherly, and divine goodness and mercy, without any merit or worthiness of mine at all!

Do you sense Luther's wonder and thankfulness for all that God is doing? This world is filled with the activities of God, and we all receive the results of God's work every day. Completely apart from anything we do or deserve, God continues to work in the world that God created. Our gracious God did not just make this world and send it on its way. God's love for all creation means that God is working everywhere and in everything. God is at loose in the world!

The Bible tells us much about how God works. In fact, scripture is clear that God's work is not random involvement. God's movement in the world is filled with purpose. God has a dream. God started to build that dream in creation, and God continues to work on that dream throughout all of human history. God's coming in Jesus is a centerpiece of that work. In the life, death, and resurrection of Jesus, God made clear that the dream was near wherever Jesus was at work.

Jesus often referred to God's dream as the "kingdom of God" or "reign of God." When Jesus began his ministry he announced his presence by announcing the coming of the kingdom. The Gospel of Mark records how when Jesus arrives he says, "The kingdom of God is at hand."

We cannot know everything about this kingdom—it is not yet fully present for us. But from scripture and especially from Jesus we can begin to see a lot about it. In this chapter we will look at just a few things that can help us focus on God's dream for our world. There is much more to say on this subject than will be said here.

One step to developing your own Lutheran voice will be to read scripture for yourself and add to the list things you see that are part of God's dream. Remember, this book isn't written to be the last word but to help you start adding your words to this Lutheran voice that we all share.

To try to capture a bit about God's dream for our world, I want to share a few stories of times in my life when people have helped me to see how essential God's dream is if we are to become a church renewed in mission. While I had learned the Lord's Prayer and prayed often for God's kingdom to come, like many Christians I never really had pondered the depth of that prayer or the radical idea that Jesus lifted up as so important. I have wondered that perhaps because I did not grow up in the church I had missed something. But as I've talked with Lutherans all over the country I have discovered that most of us have missed something. Perhaps we were so connected to the center of our culture that it was easier or more prudent simply to try to stay on the good side of those who run this world rather than long for a new one shaped by God's dream.

I began to hear about God's dream in a seminary class taught by the late Walt Bouman. Dr. Bouman used to tell us how important the kingdom of God was in Christian theology. A place of righteousness, peace, justice, and love, the kingdom was God's plan and promise for our world. Dr. Bouman always emphasized that while God had assured the kingdom's arrival in the death and resurrection of Jesus, that kingdom is both "already but not yet."

It is "already" in the sense that God has promised the kingdom to us and brought it about in the life, death, and resurrection of Jesus. It is not just some hoped-for utopia. It is a guaranteed reality. Because the kingdom of God is an eternal reality it can break into our world at any time. In faith, as we see God at work, we can already glimpse it in the present. It is already available to us. In the abundant life of Jesus, we experience this kingdom in our own lives. In acts of discipleship, we share it with others. In serendipitous ways,

God often surprises us with glimpses of the dream when we least expect it. The kingdom of God is "already."

But at the same time, the kingdom of God is "not yet." God is not finished with this world. The world is still waiting for its final fulfillment. History continues on its path and many things happen that are not yet in keeping with God's dream for the world. The tension between the kingdom being "already" but also "not yet" is the tension in which Christians are called to live.

But Dr. Bouman was very clear. The work of building this kingdom was the work of God. He called it the *missio dei*, which means, "mission of God." God had a mission and it was the end point of everything in life. Dr. Bouman's commitment to this idea and his clarity about it struck me as something I had never heard before— something totally new. I would never think of Jesus' parables that begin, "The kingdom of God is like . . ." in the same way again. God was up to something big, too big for us to grasp without stories and images to give us clues, but something really big. God was at work in the world!

A second time I remember being struck by the importance of the kingdom of God happened a couple of years after seminary. My wife Marlene and I were new to many aspects of our lives. I was a new pastor. Marlene had just finished graduate school and was a new social worker. Our daughter Erin was about a year old and we were new parents.

We attended a summer outdoor Christian festival in Pennsylvania for our vacation. The Friday night keynote speaker was a man named Tony Campolo. He gave a talk that night that he had given many times, and it continues to be a crowd favorite when he speaks, even today. That talk, "The Kingdom of God Is a Party," made both Marlene and I think in a new way. The kingdom about which Walt Bouman had taught us now took on increased importance.

One story in Campolo's talk that I will never forget was about a time when he was in Hawaii for a speaking engagement. (I want to know how to get invited to a gig like that!) Due to the time change, Tony woke up in the middle of the night. Getting up to go for a walk, he ended up in an all night diner frequented by all sorts of all-night people, many of whom made their living on the street.

Two female prostitutes came in for a coffee break. Tony overheard one say to the other that it was her birthday tomorrow and that she had never had a birthday party. After they left, Tony and the owner planned to throw her a party the next night. When the two women returned the next night for their coffee break a cake had been made, a crowd of people had gathered, and the party was on!

Of course there are a lot more details in the story than I relate here. What I want to communicate is how much impact hearing this story had on Marlene and me. God's dream includes celebrations for people who have been given little to celebrate. Those who are poor or outcast or forgotten in this world are a priority in God's dream, and when the kingdom is present they are included. A commitment to God's kingdom means a commitment to justice now. God's dream is to include everyone, and God pays special attention to those whom the world leaves out. Although I often do not act as justly and inclusively as I know God wants, I no longer can consciously think about God's kingdom without knowing that God is dreaming of a just world where no one is left out.

I think that as Lutherans, although we hear the parables of Jesus say again and again, "the kingdom of God is like . . . ," we may have been lulled into taking God's dream for granted. Jesus has to use stories to tell us about it because we only get glimpses of it. It is too radical for us simply to imagine and get it right. Each week as we pray the Lord's Prayer we say, "thy kingdom come, thy will be done, on earth as it is in heaven." We are praying for radical transformation of our world. We are urging God to finish the work—to let God's love rule and have peace and justice and mercy reign once and for all.

It may be that I am just a slow learner. As I look at Martin Luther's *Small Catechism* I now see how important the kingdom of God was in Luther's thinking. Why didn't I get this in confirmation class and why wasn't I teaching the kids about it in the confirmation classes I was leading? Luther understood the importance of the kingdom of God. Regarding the petition that God's kingdom come, Luther wrote, "God's kingdom will indeed come without our praying. . . ." Luther knew that God has a dream and that in Jesus that dream has come true. He understood that it is not up to us to make it happen. In fact, we can't make it happen. It is God's kingdom. It is God's mission to make it happen. God gives it as a gift. We receive it as a present. God's dream is the reason that Jesus came and lived among us, died at the cross, and rose again. God's commitment to this kingdom would not be stopped, even by human rejection and death.

Now seeing that God is not just into minor repairs but is committed to a world that will not be finished until the whole dream is in place, I have started to include more and more of this in my own preaching and teaching. In one sermon I gave on the Lord's Prayer, I remember challenging the congregation to change how they included the Lord's Prayer in their daily prayers that week. To better focus on God's dream, I urged them to pray the prayer slowly. When they got to the petition, "thy kingdom come, thy will be done on earth as it is in heaven," I asked them to stop, pause, and repeat the line before moving on. A few weeks later, Jeanne, one of my role models for her deep devotional life, said to me, "I tried stopping after I prayed about the kingdom and then prayed for it a second time. It really changed the whole prayer for me."

Life changing ministry begins when we help people to hunger for what God is up to rather than simply settling for getting by with what we can do. It is God's mission that sparks everything else, even for those of us who have been in the church for a long time!

Helping people to see that God's mission is so central to what it means to be the church puts us in a whole new place as we talk to people who are not in the church. I was raised by loving parents who were not too interested in church. They always thought there were better ways to spend their Sundays than sitting in church. In their defense, I think we do waste a lot of time in church working on things that God thinks are trivial, while huge things such as people's faith, living conditions, educational opportunities, health care, and broken relationships often get neglected. In addition, the most visible Christians my parents see come from two camps. One camp is the televangelist group who often spend more time preaching about what they hate in this world and who they hope God will smite next. My parents see these people as greedy nutcases of whom they want no part. The other group is opposed to talking about evolution, suspicious of public education, and seems to be opposed to progress and to life moving forward. My parents see them as wanting to restore the past and standing in opposition to much that seems to make sense to my parents. This group's political entanglements and controlling desires make my parents suspicious of them. Neither group represents anything with which my parents want to be associated. And again, I agree with my parents. These most prominent Christians don't represent me most of the time either.

Although my parents remain unchurched, they are great people with deep values and I enjoy talking with them. One evening I was talking to my dad on the phone. We mentioned the two camps that dominate much of the public's impression about the church. We began to talk about the church and its role in the world. I shifted the subject to God and God's role in the world. I began to talk about the ministry of Jesus and what it was that Jesus was committed to. I remember saying how diverse the church really is—that even though those two camps dominate the news they don't fully represent the church that Jesus came to start. In spite of a lot of differences of opinion about a lot of things, all Christians seem to have at least one thing they agree on. Everyone says the Lord's Prayer. I recall telling my dad, "When every person in the church says the words, 'Thy kingdom come, thy will be done on earth as it is in heaven', they are praying for a radical overhaul. Anyone you talk to will admit that

God's kingdom has not yet been fulfilled and that no matter how golden a past memory may seem, it was not the ultimate fulfillment of God's dream. Every person will admit that they are praying for a future that surpasses anything they have experienced in the past. Every person will admit that life can only be lived forward. In short, Christians can only be faithful if they pray for a radically new future because that's what Jesus was committed to."

I will never forget my dad's response. "Hmm. I never thought of it that way before."

The truth is, many of us in the church have not spent enough time thinking about it that way either. The church needs to spend more time recognizing that God is on a mission to bless and love the world. That mission will be fulfilled when God's dream is realized and the kingdom of God is complete. As Luther reminded us, it is coming whether we pray for it or not. God's work and God's dream will always be bigger than the church. God's work will always include doing things that surprise even those who seem to have the deepest faith. It is God's work and God is doing it. We can only rejoice and respond.

In the end, to discover our Lutheran voice we will need to remember that mission is not prescriptive but rather descriptive. It is not our work to tell God what to do. A Lutheran voice does not legislate what we are to do as if mission were simply another law piled up on all the rest. It is God's dream and we cannot prescribe when or how it will happen.

Rather than being prescriptive, a Lutheran voice is descriptive. Through the eyes of faith the use of our Lutheran voice is to describe what God is doing—to see it and announce it. Claimed by Christ, we see God at work. My wife Marlene calls these glimpses of God at work "kingdom moments" or "little flowers." It is our privilege and our joy to see what many people miss—that God has a dream for our world and that God is loose, out there in the world, already making it happen!

For Reflection and Discussion

Read Acts 1:1-5 and Acts 2:14-24. What do you learn about God's dream from these verses?

Pray, *God of creation, you are one whose dream has shaped the world and holds its future. Help us to see what you see and to bear witness to what you do. We have looked for you in the church and missed much of what you have been doing in the world. We thank you for Jesus who brings us your kingdom. We ask you, what are you doing now in the community around us?*

Pause for a time of silence and listen for God's answer. Then close with the Lord's Prayer, pausing after "your kingdom come, your will be done on earth as in heaven." Repeat that part of the prayer and then continue through to the end.

Discuss the following:
1. What does your community or neighborhood look like in God's dream? Be specific.

2. What has happened in the world in the last month that you believe most pleases God?

3. What is going on in the world where your congregation serves that makes God sad?

4. Who is God using to change the sadness to gladness? Who is at work on that which concerns God most?

4

The Church—God Prefers Not to Work Alone!

If God is loose in the world working to bring about the kingdom of God, one thing is certain: If we are going to be intentional about offering our help, we have to be able to see what God is up to. When Martin Luther wrote, "God's kingdom will surely come without our praying for it. . . ." he didn't stop there. His confidence in the work of God was his starting point, as it is for all Lutherans, but he also recognized how important it is that we connect to it with our lives. So Luther finished the phrase by saying, "but we ask in this prayer that it may also come to us."

Luther understood that God was in charge and could handle the issues facing the world. In fact, if Lutheran theologians are accused of anything, it probably is that we trust God to do the job too much and forget how important it is that we get involved. Often we have been suspicious of people who've said we need to do something. That sounds like a new law to us, and for the sake of grace we often have stayed our ground rather than forge new trails into the future.

As I write this manuscript, Dietrich Bonhoeffer would have been one hundred years old this year. As a Lutheran pastor and theologian during World War II, Bonhoeffer risked his life and eventually was killed for his efforts as a witness to God's action in the world. He brought a vision of a new kind of Lutheran church in the midst of a war where many fellow Lutherans simply stayed quiet and went along with the center of their culture. Unfortunately, Hitler stood at the center, and by refusing to find their own voice, many Lutherans missed the chance to be a part of God's kingdom as it wrestled with the powers of this world.

Bonhoeffer's view of the church was grounded in a deep love for what God was doing in Jesus. Committed to grace, Bonhoeffer also wanted to be sure that we didn't take grace for granted. He dreamed of a church that did not exist primarily to serve its members but to stand as Christ's body, committed to being a part of manifesting God's dream. In *Letters and Papers from Prison* (London and New York: SCM Press and Macmillan, 1959), Dietrich Bonhoeffer wrote, "The church is the church only when it exists for others"(p. 382).

Bonhoeffer also believed that the church needed to rethink how it worked in the world. Having spent too much time aligned with the culture of the day, the church had lost its voice. *In The Cost of Discipleship* (New York: Simon and Schuster, 1995), he wrote, "It is becoming clearer every day that the most urgent problem besetting our Church is this: How can we live the Christian life in the modern world?" (p. 55).

God's dream includes not only a different kind of world for us; God also is dreaming of a different kind of church to exist along the way. If we thought we could take faith for granted in a previous age, it is more and more clear that today's church needs to be serious about faith and see itself as an ally with God rather than a religious servant for the culture. And it is more and more clear that even though God can finish the work of the kingdom alone, God wants us to help. I'm going to write that again: God wants us to help!

As Lutherans it is essential to be sure we get the verb right in that sentence. God doesn't need our help. It isn't up to us. It never has been and it never will be. As much as we often try to play God, the outcome of all of this was known before creation, announced fully to the world in the life, death, and resurrection of Jesus, and is promised to us and received by faith. We may experience some bumps along the way, but it isn't because God needs directions. God does not need our help.

But the God revealed in Jesus is a relational God. God wants to love and be loved. By the end of his ministry Jesus had developed such a close bond with his disciples that he was able to call them his friends. But notice how the friendship is tied to the mission of Jesus, "You are my friends if you do what I command you" (John 15:14). To be a friend of Jesus is to participate in his work and to find ways to be useful to God.

Even though God can do this without help, God prefers not to work alone. Jesus wants our help. In fact, I believe that the reason God made the world the way it is was so we could be invited to help put the final touches in place—not because we have to but because God wants us to. Much as a parent rejoices when a child says a first word or takes a first step, God rejoices when we are loved into the image of God more fully and participate in what God is doing.

My friend Ruben often says, "God is going to do what God is going to do. The only question is, do we want to be part of it or not?" Do you hear how Lutheran that is? Luther's "God's kingdom will indeed come without our praying for it" exudes the same confidence in his time that Ruben has in ours. Luther's "But we pray for it that it might also come among us" brings the same desire to be a part of God's kingdom that Ruben's words call for today. God invites us to participate. Even though God doesn't need our help, God wants us to be involved.

That's why the gift of our baptism also brings with it a call to a new life. Each of us who are blessed with faith is transformed by that faith. According to Article VI of the Augsburg Confession, that transformation is called "new obedience." It isn't the old law where "if you do this, then God will do that." According to that law, we act and God nails us for our mistakes. But the new obedience is "because God has done this, therefore you are free to do that." In this gospel way of living, it is Jesus who gets nailed (to the cross) and we are freed to respond in gratitude for what we have received. God acts first. We respond because of the gift God has given.

This freedom to be useful to God is the basis for the church. God has called forth, through faith, a group of people to live out this new life. The church is simply the gathering of people who have been claimed by faith and are in the midst of having their lives changed by the power of the risen Christ working in their lives. Ideally, it is people who know what God has done for them in Jesus and who desire to be useful to God in response.

One person who helped me see this new kind of church most clearly is Lesslie Newbigin, an English missionary to India. Having lived in India a long time, when he returned home to Great Britain he discovered that the British people needed missionaries as much as the people in India had. He began to wrestle with what it meant to be a church in mission in the western world. One of my favorite books by Lesslie Newbigin is *The Finality of Christ* (London: SCM Press, 1969), in which he wrote of a missional church that saw itself in a new light. According to Newbigin, to understand what it means to be a church that proclaims the gospel one needs to understand:

- The Reign of God has come near in Jesus;
- To accept it means to be able to understand and direct all of your action – both public and private;
- There is an apostolic fellowship of those who are already committed and at work;
- This is the call to you to like commitment (p. 57).

Lesslie Newbigin opened for me a new picture of the church, grounded in God's reign and calling forth life-changing commitments as disciples of Jesus Christ. No part of our life is off limits for the life-changing power of God. Going to church is not to be an activity like joining a civic organization. It is to be aligned with other disciples who are "apostolic" (which means to be sent out by the risen Christ). And it is to be an invitational way of living that invites others to join with Jesus in the work of living out God's dream.

Now be honest, the last time you went to church, did you think about the reason you were going? In a nation where only one in five people go to church, did you think about the fact that you are in a select few rather than part of a majority? In a church where less than one third of the members even show up on a typical Sunday, did you ask yourself what is important about this? And did you think about the people gathered there with you as fellow allies in the work to participate in what God is doing?

The reason God made the church was to call forth a community of allies. The church is people like you and me who gather regularly to remind one another of what God has done for us in Jesus. We share in the Lord's Supper to celebrate God's presence in our midst. We nurture one another and share stories of how God has worked through us during the previous week. We teach each other what we've learned, pray for each other, and then God sends us back out into the world remembering that although God is present when we gather, God is loose in the world. Most of what God is up to is out there!

A primary point of being the church together is to refocus us when we gather so that we can be effective when we are apart. We don't gather to escape the world. We gather to be sure we are doing a good job of engaging it! God wants our help. If a church is doing effective ministry, people leave better prepared to be missionaries to the world and ambassadors for Jesus.

Our participation in this work is called our "purpose." An important point in this chapter is to clarify between "mission" and "purpose." Mission is what God is up to. It is the mission of God. Ultimately, Lutherans are very clear that the mission belongs to God. Everything that is of ultimate importance and eternal value starts and ends there. But that doesn't mean that God prefers to work alone. In fact, God has demonstrated time after time that God prefers to work with others—to include people in the creative work of bringing in the kingdom.

God doesn't coerce us into joining in this work. The gift of faith brings with it an invitation and the freedom to reflect God's image in our lives. As God is creative in making the world, so we are invited to be creative as we are shaped by Christ's work through the Holy Spirit in our lives. Jesus reveals who we are intended to be and transforms us in faith to be his presence in the world. This is why the church is often called the "body of Christ." In faith we are connected to the risen Jesus, and he continues to work in and through us to make the kingdom of God continue to be "at hand."

The definition of our purpose is first grounded in what God is doing. I once heard someone say, "You don't need a mission—God already has one." But God is looking for allies in mission and each of us and each of our congregations has a role to play as God's dream unfolds. That role is our purpose. Mission is God's work to bless and save the world. Our purpose is our part in God's work. The mission is always bigger than our purpose. And although the general purpose for all Christians may be similar, it is essential (and freeing) to remember that we are invited to participate in carrying out only our part of the work—the whole thing isn't our responsibility. In fact, although God invites us to participate, God will find a way to get the work done whether we do our part or not. It is God's dream and it will be fulfilled.

My second call was to serve on the synod staff in the Nebraska Synod. One aspect of that work included working with a new urban ministry in Omaha. As part of that work I attended an ELCA training session for new mission developers to help them start new congregations. At the training we were invited to attend Willow Creek, a nearby megachurch, to see their new outreach service for Gen-X-aged people.

That night a pastor named Dieter Zander was the preacher. He was in the middle of a sermon series about the Lord's Prayer. His topic that night was on "thy kingdom come, thy will be done on earth as it is in heaven." It was, and to this day remains, the most powerful sermon I have ever heard. Nearly ten years later I can still outline the entire sermon (and he preached for about an hour!). Set up by a band playing U2's "I Still Haven't Found What I'm Looking For" and a film clip from *Dead Man Walking,* he emphasized how the work of Jesus was the work of transformation—a commitment to see God's will be done on earth that it might look more like heaven. Emphasizing discipleship, Zander underscored how the gift of faith brings with it a desire for God's dream to come true. The words brought with them a renewed passion and deeper insight into the radical nature of the work of Jesus. Jesus was not about fine-tuning this world to get the bugs out. Jesus was about radical commitment to a world marked by peace, love, justice, and the things of God. And God's people were called to be residents of that kingdom now even as the world waited for its fulfillment. Walt Bouman's "already but not yet" took on new meaning. It was not just a way of understanding the kingdom of God. It was to become a way of life.

We have said already that Jesus understood a major emphasis in his ministry was the coming of the "kingdom of God." He often stated that it was "at hand" as he taught what he was doing in his ministry. As a group, we Lutherans often struggle to see God at work. We know what God did: God created the world and then came to save it through the death and resurrection of Jesus. We know what God will do: God will take each of us to heaven when we die and Jesus will come again to usher in the kingdom of God. We have down moderately well the past tense of God's work and the future tense of God's work. But often we are not as clear or confident about saying what God is doing right now. It is in the present that we struggle. But Jesus' ministry is focused heavily on living now, and he spends much of his teaching time helping us to worry less about the future (it is in God's hands anyway) and be more engaged in the present.

If we are going to join in with what God is doing, it helps to have some insight into just what it is that God is up to—not just way back when or sometime in the future, but right now in our midst. We know that God is at work in our world and we have seen that God prefers not to work alone. To find our Lutheran voice, we will have to begin to talk about how we can help.

For Reflection and Discussion

Read Acts 1:6-8, 1:38-47. As you read these passages, what do you understand about the purpose of the church?

Pray, *Lord of the church, you have formed us as instruments for you to use in proclaiming your kingdom. We confess that we have missed many opportunities to witness and to serve and ask your forgiveness. Now we come to you and ask, how can you use us now?*

Pause for a time of silence and listen for God's answer. Then close with the Lord's Prayer, pausing after "your kingdom come, your will be done on earth as in heaven." Repeat that part of the prayer and then continue through to the end.

Discuss the following:
1. Think back over your congregation's history. What things have happened that have contributed notably to God's dream?

2. Think back to the last chapter and what you sensed God doing in your community or neighborhood. With which of these things are you most involved? With which of these things could you become involved?

3. Who do you see doing God's work around you (whether they are Christian or not)? How can you partner with them to work together for God's kingdom?

5

Looking for a Vision

Vision is hard to see. I remember when high definition televisions first came out and I heard what they were supposed to do. I remember remarking to my wife, "That sounds like all it is going to do is make the wrinkles on the newscaster's faces easier to see. I can't imagine that's worth much."

Then I saw a high definition plasma TV in an electronics store. Wow! I had no idea that colors would be that much brighter and details and depth could be that much more real. I was shocked to find that things that had looked fine on my old set could really look that much better. Only when I had seen high definition with my own eyes was I able to make sense with the vision that someone had described to me.

The story doesn't end there. Living in a large metropolitan area, our family gets a fair number of television channels with the antenna in the attic. As such, we don't subscribe to cable TV. Even though a few channels are a bit snowy, not spending all that money on cable allows us to cover other priorities (like tithing). We promised ourselves that we would not get a high definition television until the old TV broke. (I still drooled every time I saw high definition sets in the electronics store and I was not above praying for the old set's demise!).

Recently the old television gave up the ghost and it was time to look at new ones. We headed to the store. We looked at prices and options and talked with the salesperson. We went home and checked out the Internet to look up prices and reviews of various sets we had seen. In the end we went back to the store and brought home the lowest priced 32-inch high definition set in the store.

Having already viewed the set in the store we knew we would like the picture. Our only question was, "Since we don't get cable, would the channels that came in a bit snowy on our old set have strong enough signals to give us a decent picture on the new set?" My fear was that finally we would be forced to get cable service in order to get a good picture.

We put the new set where the old one had been, plugged it in, and attached the antenna cable. The last step was to push the scan button to have the digital tuner find which channels we would receive over the air. It was the moment of truth. Would the signal be strong enough to support the new picture? Imagine our joy when channel 2 (always fuzzy before) came in crystal clear! But then we saw that channel 5 had multiple broadcasts—the programming on 5.1 and a weather channel on channel 5.2 (who knew there was a channel 5.2?). Channel 7 was now 7.1, 7.2, and 7.3—all products of the local ABC affiliate and all with different programming. Channel 9.1 was our old channel 9 and 9.2 was a music video station. Public television now had three signals all with different programs. The list went on and on. Where had these channels been before? We once got seventeen channels—some fuzzy. Now we had twenty-six and all were crystal clear!

What we discovered was that there is a whole new world out there that we couldn't access through our old set. Many stations had both an analog and a high definition version that were the same programs but different signals. But in addition, many stations carried additional programs that were on digital signals only. Only with the new set could we find the new stations.

This story reminds me that often, even when we think we have things figured out, the outcome is not what we expect. Vision is always incomplete. I am a relatively visionary person, but no one had explained the new world of high definition signals well enough for me to see what I was getting into. Only as I experienced it happening could I really see and understand what was going on.

Paul reminds us that "we see in a mirror, dimly," and that only when God's future is complete shall we "see face to face" (1 Corinthians 13:12). None of us sees the future fully. We all need help. The key is to recognize the future when it arrives. In this book, purpose and guiding principles give us a lens through which to view things as life happens. The idea is not to forecast the future as if one has a crystal ball but to train our eyes to see the present as clearly as possible in the light of a future that has not yet come.

This truth about vision being hard to see is a key to finding a useful Lutheran voice. As I work with congregations, it is clear that more than half the population doesn't have significant ability to process images that are as yet unseen. Most people overwhelmingly prefer using more concrete communication. In many settings where renewal is needed, the vision has long since faded and is all but non-existent. The need for vision means that often the most visionary people have already left the congregation to find a congregation with vision elsewhere. This means that often an even higher percentage of the remaining congregation is likely to struggle to see God's vision clearly. For this reason, good leadership will help make certain keys to the vision as clear and concrete as possible.

I learned this truth early in my ministry. When I interviewed for my first call there was a lot of talk about the need to reach out. We had a huge building with an almost cathedral-like sanctuary. With seating for five hundred people and average attendance of about forty-five, you can imagine how everyone longed for more people to attend worship. As we talked about this, it became clear that the remaining members wanted more young people, especially children, to be a part of the church.

We began to work on this immediately. I arrived in late spring and we decided to hold vacation Bible school in August. That gave us enough time to plan our work and prepare for kids again. It had been a while since there had been VBS. Some of the healthiest and active members agreed to help lead a class of younger children and I taught a group of older elementary kids. We advertised in the neighborhood and actively recruited kids to attend. As a result we spent the week with more than thirty children in our building, learning about Jesus and having fun. It was a great start to building relationships with children again.

That fall we resumed Sunday school. It had been a few years since there had been Sunday school classes for kids. (It had been a few years since there had been any kids.) Because none of the older members were willing to commit to teach kids, I taught an all-ages elementary Sunday school class. We had kindergartners mixed in with sixth graders. Eventually a couple of junior high kids came too. Suddenly we had over a dozen kids on Sundays. The dream of having young people, especially children, in the church again was coming true!

What happened next surprised me. Because of the small size of our congregation and the relational nature of our ministry, we were able to get a high percentage of the kids who came to Sunday school to come to worship. We added a children's sermon and soon there were kids in the sanctuary. That's when the trouble began.

Most of the children walked to church on their own. In the majority of cases the parents were not coming—they didn't even have an interest in the church. Some of the kids only had one parent at home or were in foster care or living with an aunt or grandparents. The kids were racially diverse and economically different than the white, working class group that formed the core of our congregation. With no parents to sit with them, the kids were kids when they came to worship. They fidgeted, made noise, moved from seat to seat, and got up to go the rest room right in the middle of the sermon. What had started out as a dream was turning into a nightmare for some of our older members. "Who invited these rambunctious kids to church anyway? And where are their parents? Don't they have any respect for the church?" The noise and distractions were just too much. We ended up with a fight, all because the dream we had articulated had come true. Why?

I have discovered the reason we ended up with chaos rather than joy. The majority of people who talk about the future can only envision it by using building blocks and images from their past. Only a small number of people actually can see things in their minds that they have not previously seen with their eyes. The rest of us use images from our past and rearrange them to try to imagine what the new thing might look like. This meant that while I was envisioning a variety of kids from different races and economic backgrounds and family situations, most of the remaining members were remembering the church when it had more children. In their minds they did not see a new 1989 (the year this was happening). In their minds they saw 1959 and pews filled with kids in their Sunday best sitting next to parents who had brought them and would help them sit still and be quiet. The new reality didn't look like that. They had thought they wanted more young people in church, but this felt like a bait and switch. And that angered people.

To do God's work, we need tools to help all of us see. Some in the congregation may see more clearly than others, but none of us can see the future exactly as it will be. So to help us all see enough to discuss and discern together, I suggest the following understanding of vision:

Vision = Purpose + Guiding Principles + Time

Purpose: All Christian mission is grounded in the mission of God. In fact, it must be remembered that it is God's mission, not ours. Claimed as the body of Christ for the world, the church is then sent forth as instruments of this mission. Each ministry must own the mission of God in its own context. Chapter 6 will focus on this aspect of the work.

Guiding principles: These are core values expressed in missional form. Owning the purpose will most likely come first. In many cases some visionary people will also be able to start discerning the vision.

In addition, the context, prayer, and scripture will lift up certain priorities and values that the congregation needs to commit to in order to begin to act like its future. These values are then expressed as guiding principles for the ministry. When major decisions are made, these guiding principles and the congregation's purpose can be used to weigh options and to keep the ministry on track and making healthy decisions. Chapter 8 will help you to begin to construct these in your setting.

Time: Vision is always God's dream for our future. It is a product of time. A congregation's vision takes time and energy. This means a congregation needs to be assertively and actively engaging the world around it using the purpose and guiding principles that we have developed. At the same time, the congregation's leadership needs to have the wisdom and the patience to be able to wait. This tension between pressing forward and waiting patiently is one of the most important aspects of leadership. Push too fast, and you can burn out or bowl over people in ways that are not helpful. Relax too long, and complacency and a loss of momentum results in moving from a missional mode back to maintenance, from which it can be difficult to restart.

The insight brought by this method of renewing the core of our congregations is that while some will discern and see a vision early, most people will struggle to see anything that is truly new. But for everyone, even the most visionary among us, the vision will emerge when our purpose and guiding principles are lived out faithfully and with accountability over time. Therefore we will spend the rest of our time on tools that can be useful to more of us in this work, namely purpose and guiding principles. Remember that vision, purpose and guiding principles are God directed and spiritually discerned through prayer, Bible study, community discussion, and leadership. They are the pieces that will help you develop your own unique Lutheran voice.

For Reflection and Discussion

Read Acts 9:1-19. Ananias was skeptical and could not see a vision of Saul as an ally. How do you think it felt to be asked to do something for which you could not see the outcome? Have you ever felt that way?

Pray, *God of the future, you have a dream that we often struggle to see. Often you call, and we resist out of fear or blindness. Give us eyes to see what you are doing and faith to follow, even when we are not sure where you lead. Where would you have us go now that we are not yet ready to follow?*

Pause for a time of silence and listen for God's answer. Then close with the Lord's Prayer, pausing after "your kingdom come, your will be done on earth as in heaven." Repeat that part of the prayer and then continue on through to the end.

Discuss the following:
In this chapter we will write before we speak. Give everyone three self-adhesive notes and ask, "If God has God's way with our congregation for five years, what do you see in our future?" Instruct everyone to work in silence and to not use any comparative terms (more, less, younger, older, etc.) in their answers. When everyone has written one answer on each of three different notes, have them stick them to the wall. Group like notes together into clusters. Label the clusters. Now you can talk about what you see! Enjoy!

6

Developing and Using a Purpose Statement

When I first began practicing parish ministry in the 1980s, mission statements were all the rage. Everyone was recommending that congregations have one. The advice was that they be clear and memorable, short and to the point. There were various specifics, but everyone agreed that whatever you came up with should be simple and serve almost like a tagline for a brand. When people heard the statement you wanted them to immediately think of you—much as people think of Coca-Cola when they hear someone sing, "It's the real thing."

Within this mindset, the primary reason to have a mission statement often was related to marketing the church. The idea was that the statement would allow the congregation to be easily remembered and associated with the words. Although I am going to counter this mindset in the remainder of this chapter, I will be the first to admit that this use for a statement is valid, but not primary.

The primary reason to have a purpose statement is not to communicate memorably with the world. The primary reason is to remind ourselves of what we are here for. We clarify and focus on our purpose so our ministry can stay centered on what we believe God wants us to center on. When we lose our center we struggle in our ministry. Even if the words are catchy, when people come they find that we don't live up to them. Ministry becomes a sort of membership recruitment enterprise. People come thinking that their lives will changed. If our purpose statement is not sincere and at the center of our ministry then the church ends up being just another bait and switch activity. We promote our church as one thing, yet when people come they discover we are really something else.

In spite of now knowing this, I have to admit that I learned it the hard way. I arrived at my first call excited to take on the challenge leading a congregation in renewal. I had worked on being a missional pastor and I loved a good challenge. It seemed that my first call was going to be a lot of fun.

What I found was that people in that first congregation were at various states of readiness for renewal. Some were hungry for a new kind of church life and excited about the chance to see it come about. Others were deeply committed to the previous kind of church life and worked very hard to see that nothing significant changed. What I thought would be fun turned out to be hard and often frustrating work. Some days it was hard to see the steps forward at all. Some days backwards seemed like the only direction we moved.

One moment of apparent triumph happened when we put together our first mission statement. One of the first things that I worked with leadership to do was to write a mission statement. I didn't have a lot of experience or insight into the matter. I just knew I was missional and that I wanted the congregation I served to be missional. During seminary I had been blessed to work for the Institute for Mission in the USA and Wayne Stumme was both my boss and a mentor to me. Wayne had helped me to see the importance of mission. In the work I did with him I would help assess struggling congregations for the Institute. One thing was clear, every congregation that I saw struggle also lacked a clear sense of mission. Missional thinking matters!

We approved the mission of our congregation as "Sharing the love of Jesus with all people in the Hilltop." I was pleased with the work. The statement was clearly Christian and centered in what God was doing in Jesus. It was contextual (the Hilltop was the urban neighborhood where our church building was located). It was gracious—what could be more gracious than sharing the love of

Jesus with all people? And it was active—it was our mission to share. And it met the test of being short and memorable. As far as I could tell, the statement met the criteria for everything that I had learned up to that point and even today I think it was a fine outcome.

Looking back, however, I now see that although I had some idea what I thought we were doing, the congregation was not involved. Even though the council had unanimously approved it at a council meeting, not everyone was on the same page. We had not prayed together about it. We had not studied scripture together. And we had not engaged in dialog to flesh out what it was that God was asking us to claim about our work. Most of the congregation didn't even know the statement existed when we approved it.

As good as the statement looked on paper, it lacked all three of the essential elements of transformational work that we are using in this process—prayer, Bible study, and dialog. Without these things even good work has difficulty sinking in and being owned. It might have been a good statement, but it was created using a lousy process. I did most of the work myself, explained it clearly, and asked them to sign off on it. That got us a statement but not ownership. And mission without ownership is not a mission—it is simply lip service.

It was not long after we had approved the purpose statement that our fall stewardship campaign arrived. I don't remember a lot about what I said in the sermon the day we collected our estimate of giving cards. But from a reaction I got after worship, I know I mentioned tithing as a commitment that my family had made and one that I hoped the people in the congregation would consider as well.

After worship that day nearly everyone had left the building. I was getting ready to leave when George stopped me in the hallway staircase. George didn't like change in the church. George was tall, about 6' 6", and he liked to use that height to his advantage. When he stopped me on the stairs he stopped one step above me. With the height difference it was like getting stuck in the front row of an IMAX movie theater.

"Pastor Daubert," said George angrily. "If you would get out there and do some evangelism you wouldn't have to come after us for our money."

What I discovered was that by rushing to approve a purpose for our congregation we had really not found our purpose at all. The words were nice but we hadn't wrestled with them, prayed over them, studied scripture to discern them, or talked about them with each other. The council simply had spent part of a meeting approving what sounded like a good thing. But the purpose of our struggling, inner city church was really still the same as it had been before we adopted it: "To keep the doors open and the bills paid."

Even though we had said we wanted to share the love of Jesus with all people in our neighborhood, for George the transformation of truly owning a new purpose had not yet come. Our purpose identified people as needing Jesus and as recipients of Christ's love. But for George (and I would find out later for some other people as well), reaching out to people was not first about loving them with the love of Jesus, it was about increasing the number of people who put money in the offering plate. People were reduced to a source of income. The more these unchurched people would pay, the less we in the church would have to contribute ourselves. If the pastor would bring in enough new people to pay the bills, we would not have to increase our own giving.

Years later, I feel it is important to be a bit fairer to George. He was not the only person in the congregation who thought this way. In fact, this way of thinking was not unique to that parish. As I work in renewal of congregations throughout the ELCA, I discover that most congregations that have reached a plateau or are in decline do not make serious adjustments to their ministry to be more effective until they are also no longer able to pay their bills. Two bills in particular seem to loom large: keeping the building and paying the pastor. Too many congregations lack a missional impulse at the heart of the church. Outreach becomes important only when we run low on money. When the bills are getting paid, many in our pews (and pulpits) seem willing to coast.

Accepting responsibility for the church is our job. It's not the job of those outside the church. The first step in renewing a congregation is for the people of the congregation (all of them preferably, but the leaders for sure) to say, "This issue belongs to us. We accept the challenge of being a new church in a new day. We want to take up a life of discipleship. We want to be useful to God." Without that, no congregation is likely to do much but whine and decline.

A Better Way

Despite being a slow learner, in my current parish I was willing to go deeper and move more slowly. It isn't that I am more patient this time. But I have seen that rushing through the work of this process may end up with a fine purpose statement but may leave so many people out of the process that adopting it is an illusion—God's purpose for the church still isn't etched in the hearts of God's people.

At Zion we started by planning a Saturday retreat for the church council and any other members who were willing to come. The assignment was to spend a full day digging into the book of Acts and dreaming about what God was dreaming up for our congregation. I was excited as I looked forward to the day.

The day for the retreat came and the time to begin arrived. Counting my wife Marlene and I, only ten people were present. To be honest, I was disappointed. I had done this work with other congregations and had enjoyed working with larger groups and, frankly, I had hoped for more people to come. But the ten who were there were enthusiastic. And they were the base on which the work would build. So after opening with devotions, we spent the morning in small groups digging into the book of Acts.

First we divided the large group into three groups of three or four people each. Each group was to use the three tools for transformation that we are using in this book: prayer, scripture study, and dialog. The groups were to open their time in prayer, asking God for guidance and insight as they studied the Bible. Next, each group was to read an assigned chapter from Acts together, out loud. Finally the groups were to engage in dialog about the text, centering their discussion on three things: what they saw God doing in the text, what they saw people of faith doing in the text, and how they could articulate the lessons for the church today. Each small group would then finish this part of the work by drafting a purpose statement for the church, based on the chapter they had studied.

The morning concluded with each group sharing with the others the work they had done and posting everything on sheets of newsprint on the walls of the fellowship area where we were working. This meant we all heard what the other groups had done. It meant that we also would have lots of visual reminders of what each group had discovered. It also meant that each group became teachers concerning the chapter of Acts they had studied. Remember, the quicker you can turn students into teachers, the more everyone learns.

After sharing their work, each small group met again and wrote a purpose statement for our congregation. We used the format, "God's purpose for our congregation is _____." Each group was permitted to use up to twelve words to complete the sentence. The groups then posted their statements on sheets of newsprint and hung them on the walls.

It was a powerful morning. And although there were fewer people than I had hoped for to get us started on the journey, the energy in the room was incredible! We had a strong beginning, and we had started to develop the material that we needed to begin to unify the whole congregation around a common purpose. The work was far from done, but we were beginning to find our own Lutheran voice.

After the meeting was completed, all the work we had done was left up on the walls of the fellowship area. Because our groups worked in a space adjacent to our sanctuary and narthex, everyone who came to worship on Sunday would see what we had done on Saturday. Imagine the curiosity when people saw sheets of newsprint and little notes posted all over the walls as they came into the building. People began reading and talking about what they saw. Although only ten people had started the conversation, we now had dozens of people talking! We also transcribed all of the groups' results onto handouts and made copies for people. These were distributed to every family to take home and look over. Even if only a few had started the conversation, we couldn't leave it there. If we were going to change the church, we had to get as many people talking as possible.

The next week a small team of leaders took the results of our retreat and met to try to come up with one purpose statement that would describe what we thought had come from the work in the groups. We had all their biblical notes and each group's draft purpose statement. Although there was amazing consensus about what it seemed God was telling us as a congregation, coming up with one set of words to capture it was not easy. We wrestled for a long time until it finally clicked: "We are grounded in Christ and sent to be a blessing."

Excited, we brought the result to the council, which discussed it and enthusiastically asked that it be brought to the congregation. A series of small group meetings were scheduled, and Marlene and I invited members of the congregation to come to our house for prayer and conversation. Nearly fifty people attended those meetings—an impressive turnout for a congregation that had less than seventy-five active adult members. What had started as a retreat for only ten people had multiplied five-fold and blossomed into a congregation-wide conversation about what God was calling us to be.

It has been over three years since that group of ten people gathered to pray, study scripture, and engage in dialog about what

God was calling us to be as a church. We begin every worship service by welcoming people to Zion Lutheran Church where "we are grounded in Christ and sent to be a blessing." At a recent contest to design a new T-shirt for our congregation, every entry contributed by someone older than age ten included the statement in some way in their design. When a friend from Nebraska recently brought a youth group to our church for an exchange weekend, we asked him to be our guest preacher. He found the statement so prominent in our ministry that he ended up using it in his sermon.

The above stories give two different experiences about how to generate a purpose statement for your congregation. In the first story, I took too much of a role in defining the outcome and then got people to sign on at a meeting. It resulted in a good statement but no ownership or commitment to the work. In the second, my role was more to facilitate a process. It was everyone's job to pray about it, to study scripture, and to discuss it. Rather than the clericalism of my first effort, the priesthood of all believers was honored in the second one. Through the process, we all deepened our faith and grew more united as a community of faith. By the time we had a purpose statement we also had a sense of purpose. We were one step closer to developing our own Lutheran voice.

For Reflection and Discussion

Read Acts 14:8-18. How clear were Paul and his companions about their purpose? How did their purpose relate to what God is up to in the world?

Pray, *Lord of humanity, you have formed us in your image and called us to be your people so that your dreams could be ours as well. Help us to see your purpose for our lives and give us a common sense of purpose as your church in this place. We ask you now, what is it that we are to be most concerned with and how may we help you complete your dream?*

Pause for a time of silence and listen for God's answer. Then close with the Lord's Prayer, pausing after "your kingdom come, your will be done on earth as in heaven." Repeat that part of the prayer and then continue through to the end.

Discuss the following:
1. Does your congregation have a mission statement or a purpose statement? If so, what is it and how many people know it?

2. In your daily lives, how does what you do during the week contribute in some way to God's dream? How could you be more intentional about that in the future?

3. As you look at the purpose of the church in Acts, does your congregation live out a biblical purpose in ways that are clear and genuine? How are members of your congregation involved in your purpose?

4. Give each person in your group a piece of paper and invite each to complete this sentence with twelve words or less: God's purpose for our congregation is _____. After all have written an answer, share and negotiate to reach agreement on a single statement.

7

A Purpose Statement Isn't Enough

I now know that having a purpose statement is not enough. But I have to admit I learned that the hard way. In my first parish, I really thought we had turned a corner after we approved the mission statement of our congregation, "Sharing the love of Jesus with all people in the Hilltop." I could not have been more wrong.

Looking back, I probably felt too good about the whole thing. My first reaction to the incident in the staircase with George was to assume that it was an isolated incident. But even that would not prepare me for what was to happen next. I still believed that if I shared the statement with the congregation in much the same way I had shared it with the council then everyone would understand and be on board. It would take a little time, but with some good education surely everything would start to come together. I was certain.

My encounter with George on the church stairs had been only a month or so after we had adopted the mission statement. George had not been part of the meeting when we adopted it. As I began to think about how to get the statement out in a more visible way so everyone could see it and make it their own, I decided to decorate a bulletin board. The key was to make it visible.

I got out some construction paper and made shapes to represent buildings in our urban neighborhood. I made a paper Jesus walking though the community. I made big letters spelling out, "Sharing the love of Jesus with all people in the Hilltop." I assembled these on the bulletin board located in the narthex of our church building. As people came in the front door and walked up the steps to worship they would be greeted by the picture and phrase that was going to save our church. Our members would see it and become familiar with it. Visitors would see it and know what we were about. Once we started using the purpose statement a little bit, surely people would come around and become more missional. Once again, I was wrong.

It was a Sunday morning that seemed like almost any other. I had no idea that what was about to unfold would reshape how I looked at church renewal. The simple thought that we could develop a mission statement, promote it in preaching and throughout the community, and then people would come and get on board was to be gone forever.

One of our council members was named Kathryn. Just a week or two after my new bulletin board went up with the mission statement boldly posted she was our greeter. As a member of council, Kathryn had been in on the ground floor of our mission statement. She had been at the meeting when I had presented it. She had been in on the entire discussion. And after all, she had been part of casting a unanimous vote. Unlike George, who had not been a part of all of this, Kathryn knew and understood what was involved here. I knew that I could count on her to be on board. Wrong again!

That Sunday morning as Kathryn stood at the top of the stairs greeting people, I was on the other side of the narthex talking with someone. With people milling around before worship, I wasn't paying much attention to Kathryn. She was doing her thing and I was doing mine.

Suddenly I heard a yell. "F--- you!"

Everyone in the room turned and looked. There was Orpah. It was her first visit to our congregation. She had met me while I was out knocking on doors and had decided to accept my invitation to come to church. Having moved into the city when jobs got tight in Appalachia she was raised a rural person. Longtime residents in our church called people like her "hillbillies" or "the backward folk."

Orpah had gotten ready for church that day the way she knew how. She had on a clean cotton dress, the kind she would wear under an apron during the week in the kitchen. On Sundays she wore the dress with no apron. She had washed up and was clean and ready for worship. Confident that she should go (after all, the pastor had invited her), she strolled through the front door and walked up the front steps to the narthex. On the wall in front of her were the words, "Sharing the love of Jesus with all people in the Hilltop." Why would she expect anything but a great Sunday morning?

Apparently, Kathryn had seen her differently. Orpah's clothing and something about Orpah communicated to Kathryn "hillbilly" and a lack of respectability. She could see enough signs to know that Orpah might have fit in at a church in West Virginia or southern Ohio, but she wasn't our kind of folk.

Orpah had reached the top of the stairs and Kathryn was there to greet her. Kathryn said, "Honey, this is a respectable church. There are a lot of other churches in this neighborhood where you might be more comfortable."

And so Orpah had responded with her retort and walked over to me to indignantly share what had happened. "Do you know what that lady said to me?" (At the time I didn't, but I sure knew what Orpah had said to her!) And after telling me what had happened she walked into the sanctuary and sat down in a pew for worship. A few weeks later, Orpah brought her husband Bob, and a few weeks after that, she brought her daughter and grandchildren. We had three generations of Orpah's family in church with us. Not everyone will cuss out the greeter to get through the frontlines of the church's defense, but Orpah wasn't going to take no for an answer. We all may not have known she belonged there, but she did.

Orpah and Kathryn have long since gone on to be with God. Sometimes when I remember them I imagine them around the throne of God worshiping and singing praises. Kathryn and Orpah have adjacent seats in my imaginary picture, and Kathryn says to

Orpah, "Remember that day you cussed me out to get into the church?"

Orpah smiles and says, "How could I forget?"

"I'm really sorry I was so mean to you that morning," says Kathryn.

And Orpah smiles, "Well, I probably should have been a little nicer myself. I'm sorry I reacted so strongly. I had no idea new people were so hard to adjust to."

They both nod and smile knowingly at each other. Then they turn back toward God and sing together at the top of their voices—joining the multitudes of people gathered to celebrate the amazing God who called and redeemed them in Jesus Christ.

What I learned from this incident is one of the most important elements in this work. Changing a congregation requires that we go much deeper than just producing memorable mission statements. In fact, the reason I now call them purpose statements is to remind us that the mission belongs to God. A statement that points us to a new future is only helpful if we are also willing to own the work and let go of our old selves.

The Bible is filled with references to God making old things new. It is filled with references to dying and rising. It could not be clearer that life moves forward and that to enter God's future we must also leave our old selves behind. Lutherans and most other Christians refer to this act of leaving behind an old self and taking up a new one "repentance." It means "to turn around" or "to live life in a new direction." Luther saw repentance as a daily act for a faithful Christian. It is a privilege granted to Christians that the old us died in baptism. This allows Christians to shed our old selves and repent of our sins on a daily basis. Each day is a new chance to be useful to God, no matter how we might have failed the day before.

Congregations are no different. We are learning that they function like a living being. They have life and personalities. They can be useful to God. Or they can get in the way. If congregations are going to renew (become new again) they will need to be willing to repent (turn around in a new direction). Confession and repentance are central to the work of transformation. A congregation that wants to become healthy and vibrant will have to admit to itself and to God where it needs to let go of the old self and where it needs healing and new direction.

Our congregation had adopted a mission statement (actually the council had adopted it—the congregation as a whole just heard about it). But we had not come to grips with the fact that part of why we needed a new identity was that there were aspects of the old identity that were broken and harmful. We still thought of ministry as simply doing a better job of being what we were. It wasn't us who needed to change. We were fine. We thought that we just needed to be clearer and bolder about how we could change other people. When enough of them wanted to be like us, then they would join us and do what we do. The church would be fine.

Renewing a church is not about better methods of recruiting people who will become like us. Before we are in a position to be most useful to God, most of us need to spend time repenting of who we are. Christians need the life-changing grace of God as much as non-Christians. Luther reminded us of that often. Somehow we easily can become so enamored with our religious life and so blind to our own need for change that God finds us hard to use for mission. If we aren't open to God getting through to us, why should we expect God to get through us to other people?

In our case, sins of pride showed themselves in racism and classism. People who were most like us were seen as respectable. People who didn't measure up to certain criteria were not just unre-spectable—they actually were viewed as less than human. Do you remember that pledge to be about "sharing the love of Jesus with all people. . . ?" Kathryn could not do that with Orpah because in her mind (subconsciously) Orpah was not included in "all people." Somehow, underneath all that we had said in our purpose statement, we still had a voice whispering in our ears that said, "to be fully human means to meet certain respectability criteria." A voice like that may come from Satan, but it surely does not come from Jesus.

A Lutheran voice clings to Romans 3:23, which reminds us that, "all have sinned and fall short of the glory of God." We had given in to the culture that defines certain people as "in" and other people as "out." And rather than using faith in Jesus to define people, we had settled for the voice of culture. We had issues beneath the surface too dirty to look at. Until we could admit it and repent of it, renewing our congregation would prove to be nearly impossible.

This is why having a purpose statement is not enough. Underneath saying the right things are the values that shape our old life. These are what are revealed to be most important. They shape our culture. They determine our decisions. In order to make new decisions, we also will have to take up new values. Many of these values will be non-controversial at a conceptual level. But to actually be accountable to them will be difficult and often uncomfortable.

Without this step, however, it is difficult to gain the tools we need to navigate the path of transformation. We need to think about these values, confess the ones that prevent us from faithfully serving a useful role in God's mission, and adopt new ones that generate new decisions and encourage new behaviors. These values cannot be abstract or simply long lists of things we think are important. They must be biblically and prayerfully grounded, born out of the work of the group, and put forth in a form that reminds us of who we are to become and points to new behaviors for us to adopt as we work our way forward.

These guiding principles then will be available to us as we make decisions. They will be with us in the midst of conflicts to help us sort out which direction to go. With them, if we will use them and hold each other accountable, we have a great asset to point us toward good decisions and healthy actions. But without them, if we settle for just a purpose statement, we are left to fight our instincts with no way to recognize if the habits we have formed are helpful or harmful. We need to take time to discern new principles to guide our mission. Having a purpose statement is not enough. There is still work to do as we seek to find our own Lutheran voice.

For Reflection and Discussion

Read Acts 4:33—5:11. Here we see struggle for common commitment. What do you think was the motivation behind Ananias's and Sapphira's actions? Have you ever had similar thoughts in relation to the church's work?

Pray, *God of new life, even though we often hear your call on our lives, the ability for us to commit fully is hard. We hear voices call to us in many directions. Forgive us when we fall short and follow voices others than yours. We ask you to speak to us now. In which parts of our lives do we fall most short and where do we waiver in our commitments to you as disciples?*

Pause for a time of silence and listen for God's answer. Then close with the Lord's Prayer, pausing after "your kingdom come, your will be done on earth as in heaven." Repeat that part of the prayer and then continue through to the end.

Discuss the following.
1. Think about your congregation's life and traditions. Which of these seem to happen "just because" and not carry out God's purpose for the ministry in clear ways?

2. What values or guiding principles does your congregation have that are taken for granted but might need to be changed? Do you have any baggage that prevents God from fully using your church?

3. What disciplines and ministries might need to be added to help people go deeper in their faith lives and respond with stronger discipleship?

4. In your personal lives, where do you struggle most to remain focused and committed to being a disciple and doing God's work? What will you do to change that in the coming weeks?

8

Developing Your Guiding Principles

We now move deeper into the work of finding our Lutheran voice. Having a clear purpose is key to the process, but also important is recognizing the voices that lie deep within us. These voices are so familiar to us that we hardly hear them speak. They simply whisper quietly in our subconscious, and we tune in to them without knowing we do it. These voices are called "values." They are the things that are most important to us and the most natural about how we function. Some of them are cultivated and intentionally developed. Others simply are inherited or received without thinking about them. We may not remember where they came from. In fact, we may not even remember they are there.

A key ingredient to congregational renewal is to recover consciousness about these voices. The voices that are biblically grounded and helpful to our mission we can celebrate and continue to use. The voices that are not helpful need to be discarded and replaced with new ones that are more in keeping with the future that God has for us.

Ultimately, change happens when behaviors change. Coming up with new ideas is part of change, but real change involves taking on new behaviors. Almost all of our behaviors occur without much thought. Our goal in renewing a congregation is to focus on intentional change. We need to be as intentional as possible in assessing our actions and choosing new directions. Unless we are intentional about the new behavior, we will forget what we decided in a meeting somewhere and will continue on with our natural actions. As a result, transformation will falter.

A useful format for congregational renewal involves using guiding principles. Guiding principles articulate the things we need to remember and be accountable for in living out our purpose. To be most useful, the guiding principles we form should be statements, not single words. They should be full sentences that say things about our commitments and remind us who we are called to be and communicate that image of us to others. They are an intersection between biblical spirituality and today's choices.

Let's analyze a simple guiding principle from Kelly Fryer's book *Reclaiming the "L" Word* (Minneapolis: Augsburg Fortress, 2003). In this book she shares the stories and decisions that shaped the renewal of one congregation. Unlike the work we are doing here, the guiding principles at Cross of Glory Lutheran Church evolved in the midst of circumstances that demanded hard choices. Often conflict or intense emotion was involved. In the process of working through these situations the congregation and its leaders had to come to grips with what was most important. What was it that they valued?

The principle we will examine here is, "Everyone is welcome." It is a simple principle stated in a very succinct way. Yet even here we see more than one value articulated.

The first value is contained in the word "everyone." It may seem obvious but "everyone" means all people. (Remember my purpose statement—"all people" didn't really mean all people.) When it is stated and owned by a congregation the people are claiming to be an inclusive people. To be true to itself, the congregation must be open to all they encounter. Although Kelly's congregation was primarily white and working class, it would be equally open to people regardless of race, ethnicity, political affiliation, or economic level. If a person's sexual orientation were gay or straight they would find the same open attitude and a community that rejoices in their presence. As such, the word "everyone" demands radical inclusivity. No one can be left out.

The guiding principle also uses the word "welcome." This means more than simply stating that all people are allowed to come. The onus is on the congregation to engage actively all who respond to the invitation to come. Hospitality is another value that the congregation is claiming as its own. This means that new people from every background will be greeted joyfully and made to feel at home in the congregation.

Do you see how stating the guiding principle gives the congregation clear pictures of their new future? Had they simply listed the values "inclusivity" and "hospitality" they would not have been as clear on what they meant. They would not have claimed a behavior for their own. If they were welcoming to people from another ethnic group, they might have been able to claim being inclusive and hoped that a smelly street person would leave. But by clearly claiming everyone, there is no ambiguity. The people at Cross of Glory were crystal clear. Welcoming one person does not get us off the hook with regard to someone else. Everyone knows what the standard is.

This understanding of welcoming became important at Cross of Glory. Initially the welcome theme had been lifted up because the congregation had gotten a good deal on discontinued "The Welcome Place" materials from the denomination. However, when a lesbian couple came to church and controversy ensued, the conversation about being a welcoming place moved the congregation to ask the question, "Who do we welcome?" The materials didn't list a particular audience. After heated debate, congregation leaders eventually decided that the welcome applied to everyone. No one would be asked to leave. If some chose to leave because they didn't want to be part of a church that welcomed everyone, that was up to them, but the leadership knew what needed to be said. Welcome applied to everyone.

Another congregation I worked with eventually arrived at the guiding principle, "Everyone is welcome and invited." This adds the additional behavior of invitation. As they discussed their principles, members agreed that they wanted to do more than simply welcome those who came through their doors. They also wanted to remind themselves not to wait for people to show up. It was their responsibility to invite people to come—perhaps even people who didn't know the congregation existed.

So a simple statement like, "Everyone is welcome and invited," contains at least three values: inclusivity, hospitality, and invitation. The statement is simple and memorable. It can be incorporated easily into a list of a few other similar sentences that people can remember and refer to. Much more accessible than a list of ten or fifteen values, these five or six sentences leave less doubt about what is desirable and what standard is being lifted up. They point to a vision of new behaviors by the members of the church.

When formulating guiding principles, it is important to state them in the present tense, even though the sentences may include values that are not yet fully in place. Yes, these are behaviors in our vision for the future, but we state them in the present tense to claim the new behavior as our own. They remind us of who we are to become and help us get started now. We may not be equally glad when the smelly street person sits next to us as when a well-to-do family with children comes. We may not have invited anyone to church for a few decades (I recently heard anecdotally that the average Lutheran invites someone to church once every twenty-three years!). We may not look at all like the guiding principles we include in our list. But by putting them in the present tense, we own them. We know that from everything we can discern at this point that they are a clear part of our future.

Claiming the behavior in the present is an essential ingredient to change. Ideas are nice, but as we have already said, renewal is only real when a congregation acts differently. Change is about adopting new behaviors so our actions look more like our future than the actions we previously lived out. Over time, as we act in the present like we know we will act in God's future, we start to look more like our new selves and less like the old ones.

Remember that Saturday retreat where ten of us gathered at Zion to spend a morning discerning our purpose? We spent the afternoon looking at guiding principles. We dug back into the same chapters of Acts that we had studied that morning as we looked at the purpose of the church. Each small group was assigned to dig into scripture again. They were to work together to discern the guiding principles at work in the chapter that they had studied, using the question, "What are the five most important principles that your group sees in the chapter?"

There are two places where it is easiest to discern these principles. The first is to look at an action that seems unusual or out of character. What motivated the person or persons to do this when a typical person most likely would not? The second place to look is to see where a significant decision was made, especially if it involved some conflict or demanded courage. What ultimately was most important to the people of faith as they made this choice?

Each group was asked to find these principles, write them out on sheets of newsprint, and then teach the other groups what they had found. The format was the same as in the morning: start with prayer, look to the scriptures, and engage in dialog to reach consensus about what the group saw as most important. Once again, the act of reporting back orally turned the students into teachers as quickly as possible.

After the groups had completed their work and reported, we sent them back into small groups for one more task. By now people were getting tired. A lot of energy had been put into the work. But in order to have the last pieces that we needed to draft a Lutheran voice, the teams would need to give us one more thing. We needed them to go back and generate their proposed lists of guiding principles for Zion.

To start this portion, we asked everyone to look to all the work that had been done throughout the day. Teams were to reflect on more than the work done by their own group. Everyone's work was now to be looked at collectively. We began by taking advantage of all the input that was now posted on our walls. Sheets of newsprint held lists of things that God was up to, behaviors that disciples had offered in mission, proposed purpose statements, and lists of biblical guiding principles. There was a lot of material!

We began the last task with prayer. First we walked in silence around the room, each of us reading all that had been assembled throughout the day. Everyone was asked to remain in silence. It was time to listen to all that God had said to us already through the prayer, scripture study, and dialog of the day. The notes would remind us of what we had found and help us to see patterns that pointed to what seemed most important.

Then we had each group reassemble, pray together, and generate a list of five guiding principles they saw as defining faithful ministry at Zion. After generating this list of five suggested guiding principles, each group was told to add, "Jesus is Lord and Savior," to the list as the very first principle. This principle, which is also a creedal statement, would put all the others into perspective. It would remind us that these principles were to be set in the context of Christian faith. They were only useful in the context of honoring the lordship of Christ in our midst.

At the end of the afternoon we had three lists of biblical principles based on portions of the book of Acts and three lists of suggested guiding principles to shape our ministry. This material went to the same team of leaders who worked on our purpose statement. Their task? To review all of the principles that had been discerned—both from the Acts study and the suggested lists of guiding principles the teams had generated. They then were asked to generate a composite draft of guiding principles to be brought forward for review and discussion by the whole congregation.

Our Final Product

After the writing team had completed a draft, the work was reviewed by the congregation council. As had been done with the purpose statement, the guiding principles were brought forward for the congregation's reflection. Nearly fifty people met to discuss the purpose statement and share their thoughts about the guiding principles. These fruitful meetings helped us to talk about what was most important in the church and how we could be a part of what God was up to in our community.

Eventually, we called a special congregational meeting where one of the primary agenda items was the approval of the purpose statement and guiding principles of the congregation. The mistakes I made in my first parish would not be made again. The whole congregation voted on the purpose statement. In addition, we wrestled with biblical values and crafted guiding principles to help us shape future decisions and behaviors. The whole congregation voted on these principles as well.

A copy of the final product we approved is in the appendix. I hesitate to share it because of the human tendency to look for shortcuts. There are no shortcuts to doing this work. Your congregation will be blessed by leaders committed to praying, studying scripture, and dialoging about what it is God is up to. Simply finding the work of others and adopting it as your own cannot replace the insights, ownership, and unity that comes from working through the process for yourself.

There is a Lutheran core common to all Lutheran voices. But beyond that core there is not one Lutheran voice but a family of Lutheran voices. These voices are committed to making the gospel of Jesus incarnational—making the gospel real in the settings to which God has called us. As Lutherans we are all grounded in a faith that trusts that God is in charge and that we are in relationship with God and with each other through scripture study, prayer, and dialog. But each of us is responsible for discerning that word and speaking it in clear terms that shape our ministry and communicate how God is active in the world around us. While the work you are doing in this book will not finish that task, you are well on your way to developing your own Lutheran voice.

For Reflection and Discussion

Read Acts 10. How did Peter learn about what was most important to him?

Pray, *God of our lives, you mold us through the work of your Holy Spirit so that we can be Christ's body for the world. Help us to find what is most important to you. Shape us in your image more fully so that we love what you love. We ask you, what is it that is most important to you?*

Pause for a time of silence and listen for God's answer. Then close with the Lord's Prayer, pausing after "your kingdom come, your will be done on earth as in heaven." Repeat that part of the prayer and then continue through to the end.

Discuss the following:
1. Based on all we have done so far, what things seem to be most important to God?

2. If God were to make a list of things that God wanted your congregation to value, what would be on the list?

3. Give each person a piece of paper and ask him or her to write down five things that the congregation should value if it was an ideal, missional congregation. Have each person work alone in silence. Then discuss and try to come up with a draft list of things that should be most important based on scripture and your sense of

what God needs to do in your context. The final list should have only five or six statements. Put "Jesus is Lord and Savior" at the top of the list. Consider sharing the list with others or having several groups do this. Post the lists and be sure to talk about them!

9

How Do Guiding Principles Work?

Having guiding principles is not the same as using them. Now that we have started to articulate the principles that we believe hold some help for our future, how do they work? What does it look like to use them?

When I accepted the call to work for the ELCA churchwide organization a few years ago, it meant that my family would be moving from Omaha to the Chicago area. Living in the Chicago suburbs meant that we had to find a church. It was the first time we had to really look for a church since I had graduated from seminary. Our family had been part of the congregation to which I was called as pastor, and when I had served on the bishop's staff in Omaha we lived less than two blocks from St. Matthew Lutheran Church and felt called to participate in our neighborhood congregation. Up to this point, "church shopping" was unnecessary.

The Chicago suburbs were a new experience. The town we lived in had more than fifty thousand residents but no Lutheran congregation. There were several congregations in the neighboring suburbs that we decided to try. It was not an easy decision. With a family of four, getting everyone to agree on something is not easy! But after a series of visits to various congregations, our family all agreed that Bethel Lutheran Church would work for home base for our family.

The second year that we belonged to Bethel, Pastor Frank asked me if I would help Bethel clarify its sense of mission—perhaps doing some of the work that we did with congregations in the ELCA with the people at Bethel. I agreed and asked my wife

Marlene to co-lead a Saturday retreat for the people of Bethel in order to start the process.

The Saturday of the retreat we had a great turnout. Lots of people from Bethel had agreed to come spend a day praying together, studying scripture, and talking about what God was up to. The hope was that we could begin to discern together what God's dream for the congregation was.

We followed the same process as I had outlined with other congregations—worship and prayer, small group study, large group sharing, and finally, posting the best thoughts about what they thought God's purpose was for Bethel.

When the day was over a team of leaders took all the results and drafted a purpose statement for the congregation as well as a list of four guiding principles. That draft document went to the council members who discussed and approved the work. The leadership then scheduled meetings for people to gather again and to share their reactions to the work. After several months of good conversation and reflection everyone was in agreement. What we had was a helpful tool to remind us of what was to be most important to the people of Bethel as we made decisions to shape our congregation's future.

Because we had spent so much time carefully working through the process, when the time had come to vote on the guiding principles, I was already confident of how the vote would turn out. The Sunday of the congregational meeting I was working at another congregation. I didn't feel too bad about having to miss the meeting. The work was done. We had held lots of meetings and had hours of discussions. Unlike the work I had done in my first parish, here everyone was on board. The purpose and guiding principles would be approved—probably unanimously.

But when I came home I still wanted to hear about the outcome. Immediately I asked my wife, "How did the meeting go? Did they pass the guiding principles?"

"It was unanimous," she said. "We passed the purpose and guiding principles with a vote of 70-0."

But I could tell there was more to the story. After twenty years of marriage I didn't need more words to see that she was frustrated. Marlene went on to tell me what else had happened.

Immediately after the guiding principles were adopted, the meeting took up what to do with money from the endowment. Bethel's endowment was not large—about $26,000 was in the account. But that had dropped in value by $3000 from the year before, due to a downswing in the stock market. Still, the congregation's dividend check was for about $1800. The endowment had been set up so income each year would be distributed to care for needs in the community—it could not be used by the congregation. The money this year was to be given to support housing homeless people in local churches that took turns acting as shelters. Several of Bethel's members volunteered at nearby All Saints Lutheran Church, one of the local shelter sites.

Then someone noted that even though the dividends were for $1800, the principal had dropped by about $3000. In this member's mind, the fund had not made money that year. In fact, it actually had lost money. A motion was made that rather than giving the money to the homeless shelter this year, the dividends should be redeposited into the account to make up for the loss in principal. This might have made sense had the congregation in previous years given away increases in principal in addition to the dividends—but they had never done that.

As my wife remembered the events unfolding, there was some discussion but almost no one seemed to think keeping the money was a bad idea. Somehow, even though the congregation could never use the funds in the endowment for anything internal, keeping the money just made sense anyway (remember those subtle voices that whisper in our ears?). How could it be smart to give away dividends if the principal had dropped? When the discussion ended and it was time to vote, the congregation voted 68-2 to keep the money. Marlene, a social worker, was one of the two who had wanted the dividends to be given to the shelter. It is no fun to lose 68-2 in anything. As a social worker it made her furious to see a congregation decide not to help homeless people in order to play it safe with investments.

"Did anyone use the guiding principles?" I asked.

This was not the best response to an angry wife! "No!" she snapped. And now, realizing there was ammunition she had not used, she was even more frustrated.

Always the teacher (my pastoral instincts sometimes kick in, but it is often later in the process), I showed her how guiding principles work. The congregation had just voted that these principles are the things by which they want to be known. They had just decided unanimously that one of those is "We are God's hands and voice in the world." And so I said, "If someone simply had asked, 'Will we be better hands and voices for God if we keep the money, or will we be better hands and voices for God if we give the money to the shelter?' everyone in the room would have known the right answer. The decision might have come out differently."

Re-energized, Marlene decided that the congregation needed a way to keep the purpose and principles in front of it as it made future big decisions. She typed up a sheet with the purpose and guiding principles on our computer and brought it to a local copy center. There she had it blown up into a large poster-sized document. At its February meeting she presented the church council with the framed poster for the wall of the meeting room. Because we also had decided to re-enter parish life by becoming a ministry team at Zion Lutheran Church in nearby Elgin, where we still live, she also resigned from council at that meeting—not because she was still angry but because it was now time for the next chapter in our ministry. We had taught Bethel a lot. But we also had learned a lot. We were better equipped to help Zion because of what we had both led and learned as members at Bethel.

The above story reminds us of a key thing about guiding principles, namely that they are not ends in themselves. They are tools to be used in ministry. They lift up significant aspects of the things we believe we will value when our vision is fulfilled. But missional congregations cannot settle for just having guiding principles. Having them but not using them makes the church no more missional than owning a hammer and a saw makes someone a carpenter. Tools are just tools. They need to be used. Having them in the minutes of a congregational meeting is of little long-term value. Most of us will forget that we even did the work, much less what the outcomes were. But when a congregation uses guiding principles well, hard decisions become clearer. Things that seem important are put in perspective. No congregation with clear purpose and guiding principles should ever be seriously split over carpet colors in the sanctuary! Ideas that get debated based on people's moods, personalities, or friendships are now lifted up toward the things the congregation has discerned and owned as most important. A different way of being church is possible.

Often, the guiding principles we adopt will not seem natural for us (that's why we need them!). For example, the natural thing for many struggling churches is to hoard resources for a rainy day rather than be generous. We do this even though we know God wants us to be generous. But one of those voices from the world says, "Take care of yourself first and then help others if there is something left over." It isn't God's voice telling us to take care of only ourselves—it has no part in a Lutheran voice. We need new voices to speak to us if we are to become something different than we have been.

But if we look at scripture and claim these new guiding principles as our own, they can help us make decisions that are better for seeing God's future unfold among us. Earlier in this book we looked at Luther's explanation of the Lord's Prayer. In his *Small Catechism* he says, "God's kingdom will indeed come without our praying for it, but we pray for it in this prayer that it may also come to us." The scriptural principles discerned and owned by a community of faith can give us collective eyes to see more clearly what God might be doing and help us pursue God's mission faithfully as a church. In the process, a little bit of the kingdom may become visible and "may also come to us." Luther's catechetical prayers are answered in congregations where God's dream is at the center.

Let's go back to Bethel, the congregation that kept the money rather than giving it for the shelter, and see what a difference using guiding principles can make. A few months after our family had moved to Zion in Elgin, I was leading an outreach event for the Northwest Conference of our synod. Pastor Frank came up to me and said, "Dave, I've got something to tell you after the meeting and you have to promise to tell Marlene." There was a spark in his eye and a lift in his voice that got my attention. I was curious what he wanted to tell me. It seemed pretty exciting. This is what he had to say.

Bethel was not heavily invested in the homeless ministry. That probably was clear from the events I wrote about earlier. The Lutheran base for this work actually was at All Saints Lutheran Church across town from Bethel. While some of Bethel's members volunteered there and were very committed to the ministry of housing, many other members had very little awareness that Bethel was even involved.

In the spring, just a few months after Bethel had voted to keep the endowment dividends, All Saints voted to enter into a remodeling program. It would involve a major overhaul to much of the building. There was no way they could do the renovations and also continue to house homeless people during the project.

Leaders from All Saints approached Bethel's leadership to ask if Bethel would be able to house the shelter during the remodeling. Remember, just four or five months earlier Bethel had voted almost unanimously not to give money to the homeless shelter. Now they were being asked to house it!

The council meeting at which this was discussed went like a lot of congregation council meetings. For a while there were lots of opinions but no clear decision emerged. Some thought it was a neat opportunity and the church should host. Others thought it was a nuisance and would bring smells and wear and tear on the building. Others thought it might even be dangerous to house homeless people. Debate dragged on. People were becoming frustrated with each other and patience was wearing thin. Then one of the council members looked up at Marlene's poster on the wall. "You know," he said, pointing to the poster, "It says right here that, 'Everyone is welcome and invited.' It doesn't say 'except poor people.'"

The room got quiet. Debate stopped. The answer literally was written on the wall. If Bethel was to be true to what it believed God was calling it to become, then the answer was obvious. The council voted to house the homeless shelter, and the church started in a new direction. Being able to use and be accountable to the vision makes the unthinkable possible. In just a few months Bethel had gone from voting down making a small financial gift to the shelter to becoming a site to house the homeless. No wonder Pastor Frank was so excited!

This story illustrates an important point. Many visions are never seen until they emerge. In January, when the purpose and guiding principles were adopted, the congregation had started to claim a missional identity grounded in the discovery of their own Lutheran voice. The day they did that, not one person in the world knew that they should house homeless people. The shelter had all the sites it needed. All Saints Lutheran Church had not yet decided to remodel their building. Only a small percentage of Bethel's people were even involved in the work. But because they began to claim a voice that would shape their decisions and behaviors, Bethel was in a position to respond faithfully to the world. This is very important—a congregation with purpose and guiding principles must live them out by engaging the world around it. Remember that God is on the loose out there! To be connected to what God is up to, we need to be out there too.

Despite the fact that no one in the world could possibly have known there would be a need, Bethel had started to decide to say yes to the request it received to house people way back at that January meeting. By holding to the purpose and being accountable to their own guiding principles, over time they encountered a chance to be signs of the kingdom of God. The biblical dream of people with a roof over their head confronted them. The moment of truth had arrived.

It is not always necessary to see the outcome ahead of time. In some cases it is not even possible. But purpose and principles give us touch points for the vision. If we use them we are at least likely to recognize the vision when it arrives.

Developing your own Lutheran voice means a major step has been taken. When something comes along that distracts you from your purpose, you now have a reason to say no. But when God sends an opportunity to be the bearer of a "kingdom moment," you also have the clarity to help you say yes. In the end, saying yes to being involved in what God is up to is what developing a Lutheran voice is all about.

For Reflection and Discussion

Read Acts 16:16-40. See all the places where Paul and Silas made difficult choices. What guiding principles did they have and how did they use them?

Pray, *God of new life, through faith in Jesus you mold new people out of old ones and make all things new. Help us to be clear about what we are called to become. Grant us courage to be bold in our witness and help us stand out as ambassadors for your kingdom. Show us what we are to look like when we are faithful.*

Pause for a time of silence and listen for God's answer. Then close with the Lord's Prayer, pausing after "your kingdom come, your will be done on earth as in heaven." Repeat that part of the prayer and then continue through to the end.

Discuss the following:
1. Have you ever had a time when you knew what God was calling you to do and you "chickened out?" How did it feel?

2. Have you ever had a time when you sensed God's call and your values ran so deep that you had to respond in a bold and courageous way? How did that feel?

3. What courageous choices do you see before your congregation in the next few months? In the next year? How will you decide what is important and how will you make prayerful and courageous choices that further God's work in the world (out there!)?

4. In order to be more intentional about making missional decisions, what do you think needs to change about the way your congregation functions in the future?

Conclusion

The title of this book implies that articulating God's purpose and guiding principles will renew your congregation. The truth is that this process is one place to start renewing the core of your congregation. It is a way to engage the scriptures, to spend time together in prayer talking to and listening to God, and to engage one another in dialog about what God is calling the church to be. If you have caught a glimpse of the living God who is always on the move then you know that God does not sit still. In the coming of Jesus we have seen that God is committed to the world in which we live. God has a dream for creation and that dream is too important for God to sit still. Much about God is always fresh and new and often hidden from our sight.

So now that you have worked through starting to articulate your own Lutheran voice, it is important to remember that none of this is the last word. In the Lutheran tradition Martin Luther doesn't get the last word, he gave us the first word. The Augsburg Confession didn't give us the last word either—it added words to the foundation. After the principles are approved and the purpose statement has been memorized, be sure to keep praying, keep studying scripture, and keep having conversations about what God is doing. There is no last word that humans can say that will capture all that God is and does. A healthy Lutheran voice is always stretching to be faithful to a living God, revealed to us in Jesus Christ and active from now into eternity. Jesus Christ, the "alpha and omega," is the first word and the last word in all of this. Our task is to listen to his voice, to allow the Holy Spirit to shape us, and to articulate our own Lutheran voice so that the context to which God is sending us can hear Christ speak in fresh and meaningful ways today.

Within this book I have been careful to give only a few examples of purpose statements or guiding principles. That has been intentional. Too many of us will be tempted simply to take up the work of others rather than struggle through the hard process to develop something unique for ourselves. I am amazed at how many congregations I have come across that merely took the guiding principles from Kelly Fryer's *Reclaiming the "L" Word* and printed them up for their own congregation. The principles in Kelly's book are wonderful, and they continue to serve Cross of Glory well long after they were developed. But as I have talked to Kelly and met people who are part of Cross of Glory I have seen that more was transformed by the prayer and study and dialog that led to the principles than would have been had they just found them somewhere and copied them onto a bookmark. In fact, one reason I felt called to write this work was to build on the great work that Kelly has done. I want to encourage all of our congregations to follow in her footsteps, not by copying her guiding principles, but by building on her passion for a church that cares about what God cares about. We all need to do this work!

I have promised in this book to share the purpose and guiding principles of Zion Lutheran Church in Elgin, Illinois, where I am privileged to serve as pastor. These are not my principles. They belong to the congregation and they have come from our conversations with God. They have served us well so far, but the time may come when God reminds us that we need to say something else. While I know there is a danger of printing them, I list the work here in order to be helpful:

Purpose: "We are grounded in Christ and sent to be a blessing"
Guiding Principles:
1. Jesus is Lord and Savior.
2. Deepening our faith strengthens our discipleship.
3. Everyone is a minister.

4 God sends us as gifts to the world.
5. We love to tell the story.
6. We invite all to join us in God's work.

It is essential that after your congregation gets a purpose and guiding principles in place it doesn't assume it has been renewed. Renewal is not a goal—it is a way of life. It is grounded in the transformational power of meeting Jesus and committing to follow him. Renewal is more possible from this new spot because the work that has taken place has been a spiritual journey. This work will help to shape the congregation with a clearer understanding of its identity and role in God's work. But ideals are only dreams until leaders have the courage to lead and communities of faith have the strength to do the hard work of living these new ways of being the church. It will take the power of God at work in us to make these dreams become reality.

A book like this has focused primarily inward on the life of the church. It is true that renewal is necessary from the inside out. Before we focus on changing other people we need to be open to being changed ourselves. At the same time, the world we live in continues to change. There is a danger of looking for too long only at ourselves. Not engaging the world around us could mean that we become an increasingly irrelevant ghetto of Christians. That is what has happened in much of Europe.

God is often "out there" and we are often too concerned with getting more people to come "in here." In the process, we could miss much of what God is doing. Sadly, our good intentions could mean that others miss getting a glimpse of God at work as well. We must be equally clear: renewal is necessary from the outside in as well. A church that does not engage its world with the love of Jesus and a desire to be useful to God will never find its life. To not look out at what God is doing means that the church could miss most of what God is about! God made the church for the sake of the world.

Ironically that means that the church needs the world if it is to be the church.

Real renewal will only happen as we participate in God's work. Armed with new eyes to see, the congregation's membership will have to get outside and into the community around it. People will need to rethink their lives so that family, work, school, and all of life are reclaimed places where Christians see God at work. Most of what God already is doing has been missed by those of us who go to church. We have been too busy coming to church and doing religious stuff. In the process it is easy to forget that God has been out in the world, working in front of our eyes all along!

Renewing the church will mean meeting new people and seeing them as allies in the work of God's kingdom—not just warm bodies to recruit for membership. It will mean learning about their lives with an open curiosity. It will mean the healthiest congregations will spend less time in church buildings, trying to start programs to attract people. Instead, the church's time together will be spent celebrating what God has done in Jesus, reminding ourselves of Christ's living and ongoing presence in our lives, and equipping people to go out and change the world for the sake of God's dream.

Purpose and guiding principles help us to remember who we are, whose we are, and what we are here for while we are out there. As we engage a culture that may pull us in many directions, they help us to stay centered. Being centered helps us to share what we are about and to invite others in to what we see God is doing.

I hope that digging into scripture and spending time in prayer will remind you of how important it is to be pushed out into the world. Jesus' coming into the world was for the world. We in the church are blessed to be a part of it, and through faith we are freed to see and be invited to be a part of God's dream. When we see what God is doing, we are called to announce it and to invite others to see God's work as well. Sharing with the church and the world what God is doing through the work of Jesus is what Lutherans have been about from the beginning. To add new life to that tradition, we all need to find our own Lutheran voice. But a true Lutheran voice will not be shared only by the pastor from the pulpit when we gather on Sundays. A true Lutheran voice will shape what we say and what we do with our whole lives as we are all sent out as Christ's ambassadors and to serve as Christ's presence each day in the world.

Appendix A

Purpose and Guiding Principles

Purpose

Research has shown over and over again that those congregations that are clear about what God's purpose is for them *in the world,* are in a much different position than those that are not. This is one of the central points for renewal.

When defining congregational purpose, it is important to remember the following:

1. It is *God's* purpose, not our purpose, that is to be defined and discerned. As such, clarification of purpose is a spiritual exercise.

2. Purpose for the congregation is always related to God's purpose in the world (the mission of God or *missio dei).*

3. Purpose always includes the world as a focus. A purpose to "survive" has been shown to be unfruitful in renewal. This is in keeping with the gospel message reminding us that new life means risking or even experiencing death. The church is an instrument for God's work.

Guiding Principles (contain core values)

When a community comes to grips with its purpose, it must also come to grips with its identity. Every community has values, often unarticulated and taken for granted. A key to renewal is to claim the values of our future, the ones God desires for us. These values, articulated in missional statements, serve as guiding principles.

Guiding principles are the central things that are to be held to in all circumstances. They are the non-negotiable. By discerning them and articulating them ahead of time, they become useful in the midst of difficult decisions. It is vital to be clear about them and to agree to them, not out of a sense of legalism, but out of a desire to attain the vision that God has for us. Not everything has to be stated. What is said should be that to which it is most important to be held accountable.

Guiding principles are:

1. Directly related to the biblical values of Jesus and God's vision for the church in mission.

2 Only meaningful in the context of God's purpose.

3. Articulated in ways that will be helpful in making decisions on the journey.

4. Clear enough and few enough to be helpful.

5. Ideals to which the community agrees to be held accountable. They may conflict with current practices.

When writing guiding principles, it is best to articulate them in terms that help advance the purpose (you need to have some sense of the purpose to do guiding principles—even if you have not yet formally written a purpose statement).

More than five to seven guiding principles are probably getting to be too long to be helpful. Always be sure that "Jesus is Lord and Savior" goes to the top of the list and then develop the remainder.

Appendix B

Sample Event

Purpose and Principles Planning Retreat

This event should be done in an open manner that involves as many leaders as possible and invites others to come as well. It will work easily with relatively large groups of people by using small groups to process the Bible studies. Everyone should be told to bring a Bible to the event!

8:30 A.M.—Hymn or song, explanation of the purpose for the day, and opening prayer (15 minutes)

8:45 A.M.—Bible Study —Digging in to the Book of Acts (90 minutes total)

Use small groups. Allow 60 minutes for study and 30 minutes to report.

A. Form small groups. Keep groups smaller than eight per group. Count off by the number of groups needed, depending on how many are present. *Do not let people self-group.* There should be a multiple of three groups (3, 6, 9, etc.—usually six groups is enough) so that an equal number of groups study each chapter. These will be the work groups for the day.

B. Give each group one chapter to study. If more than three groups are formed, give more than one group the same chapter to study. *Do not give more than one chapter to any group!*

1. Acts 2
2. Acts 10
3. Acts 16

C. Have each group discuss the text. Each group will need to have a scribe to record answers to the following questions. Each group should list at least five or six answers for each question. Have them read the text and then spend about 10-12 minutes on each question. The facilitator should help them keep on track with the task and the time available.

1. What did God do in the chapter you studied?

2. What did people of faith do in the chapter you studied? (For example: prayer, public preaching, etc.)

3. What key lessons would you say any church should learn/ remember from this chapter?

D. Report back to large group. (group scribe serves as primary reporter)

1. Record all answers on newsprint, using large print and markers.

2. Process each question for each group one at a time. (For example, have the group working on Acts 2 list all the things they found God doing in their text, then have the group working on Acts 10 do the same, then the group working on Acts 16 do the same. Then move on to question 2 and repeat the cycle.)

3. Post the newsprint sheets on the walls around the room for everyone to see.

E. Close session with prayer.

10:15 A.M.—Break (15 minutes)

10:30—Purpose Session (90 minutes total)

A. Return to the same small groups.

B. Sticky Note Exercise—*This is done in silence. Do not allow any conversations until step 6!*

1. Give everyone a self-stick note.

2. Have 10 minutes of silent prayer and reflection on morning lessons—encourage people to wander around the room in silence and reflect and pray as they read the newsprint notes from the earlier session. *Maintain silence for the entire time as participants work and pray and think! No one should write until they have walked around the room and read what is posted and spent time praying.*

3. Instruct each person to create a purpose statement by completing this sentence, adding no more than twelve additional words: "God's purpose for our church is . . ." Have them write their statement on their sticky notes Remind participants to remain silent as they compete this task.

4. Have participants post their sticky notes on the wall in silence. The purpose notes from each group go in a cluster on one wall.

5. Let participants read the notes in silence until everyone has read what everyone wrote.

6. After each person has written a purpose statement for the congregation, reassemble the small groups again. Instruct each group to discuss the statements and from them produce one purpose statement to share with the large group.

7. Come together as a large group and have small groups share their draft purpose statements.

8. Save written copies of each group's statements for the leadership team to use after the retreat.

12:00 P.M. Lunch (30 minutes)

12:30 P.M.—Biblical Guiding Principles (90 minutes)
(Return to the same small groups from the morning session.)

A. Review the chapter (Acts 2, 10, or 16) that you studied earlier. Look at major events and the decisions/choices that people of faith made in them. What values or principles were they using to make those decisions? Each small group should make a list of all the key principles they see in action. Do not try to determine the most important ones; just list as many as you can in 30-40 minutes.

B. Sort through the guiding principles you have found and discuss which ones seem to be the most important. Compile a list of the five most important.

C. Bring the small groups back to a large group and have each group share the top five guiding principles that they see in

action in the Bible text. Have someone from each small group read the principles that they have discerned. (A possible idea is to have five different people from the group each read one principle. This involves more people in the reporting.)

2:00 P.M.—Break (15 minutes)

2:15 P.M.—Congregational Guiding Principles (75 minutes)

A. Return to the same small groups. Have everyone wander and read what has been posted through the day. Then have each group draft five guiding principles for the congregation. What should be the most important as you follow God's purpose for your congregation?

B. Have each group share with the larger group the five principles they drafted.

3:30 P.M.—Closing Information and Sending Prayer

Explain what will happen with the work of the group after the event (see below). Thank participants and send them home with a prayer and blessing.

After the event:

1. The leadership team will take the results of the Bible study reports and the groups' purpose and guiding principles statements, and they will meet in the week following the event to discuss the results. In most cases, the majority of what you need will have been articulated during the event. Talk about the event, purpose, and principles ideas that the groups suggested at the event/retreat.

2. Assign one or two people from the leadership team to write a draft statement of purpose and principles.

A. The purpose statement should be concise, missional, and outward in its focus, and contain both God's mission and the congregation's focus as clearly as possible.

B. Guiding Principles: These principles are statements of the congregation's hopes and ideals, not just its present realities. In most cases five or six guiding principles will underlie the hopes of the congregation. Make the first principle "Jesus is Lord and Savior." Refine, rewrite, and combine the list from the groups at the retreat. Bring them together and define five or six values to which your congregation needs to hold itself accountable.

3. Re-gather the leadership team to review and revise the draft statements. Put them in a final form to be brought to the congregation for study, discussion, and adoption. The leadership team should work very hard on this part of the process. The guiding principles and purpose need to be biblical, contextual, and helpful. They also should be short and memorable. Don't short change this step!

4. Bring the material to the congregation, usually going first to the church council and then, after approval, to the congregation as a whole. This will happen differently in each setting. The key is to show how the proposed statements and core values were derived from the biblical work and the vision work done by the congregation. Facilitate small group discussions and process the outcomes in ways appropriate for your congregation. If significant changes are proposed, do not incorporate them at the meeting. Document the changes and bring them back to the leadership team for reflection and editing.

5. When there is a final proposal and clear ownership of the purpose and principles, then approve them. This could be done at a congregational meeting or at church council, whichever seems most appropriate for the congregation. It usually is best to do this at the largest gathering practical—the congregation in a meeting if possible. The goal is to foster ownership.

6. Use the purpose and principles in ways that celebrate what has been done, help members remember them, and begin to move toward applying them. Great job getting this far!

Notes

1. To read this study, go to www.elca.org/research/reports/evan1991.pdf. There is a wealth of other great information at this site!
2. Walter Brueggemann made this statement on July 3, 1996, during a lecture for the Association of Chicago Theological School's Doctor of Ministry in Preaching program.

Additional Resources

Barna, George. *The Power of Team Leadership.* Colorado Springs: WaterBrook Press, 2001.

Bonhoeffer, Dietrich. *The Wisdom and Witness of Dietrich Bonhoeffer.* Selected and with meditations by Wayne Whitson Floyd. Minneapolis: Fortress Press, 2000.

Fryer, Kelly. *A Story Worth Sharing.* Minneapolis: Augsburg Fortress, 2004.

Fryer, Kelly. *Reclaiming the "L" Word.* Minneapolis: Augsburg Fortress, 2003.

Fryer, Kelly. *Reclaiming the "C" Word.* Minneapolis: Augsburg Fortress, 2006.

Hauerwas, Stanley and William H. Willimon. *Resident Aliens.* Nashville: Abingdon Press, 1989.

Herrington, Jim, Mike Bonem, and James H. Furr. *Leading Congregational Change* (book and workbook). San Francisco: Jossey-Bass, 2000.

Nessan, Craig. *Beyond Maintenance to Mission: A Theology of the Congregation.* Minneapolis: Fortress Press, 1999.

Powell, Mark Allan. *Loving Jesus.* Minneapolis: Fortress Press, 2004.

Sellon, Mary K., Daniel P. Smith, and Gail F. Grossman. *Redeveloping the Congregation: A How-to for Lasting Change.* Washington, D.C.: Alban Institute, 2002.

Sjogren, Steve. *Conspiracy of Kindness.* Ventura, Calif.: Regal Books, 1993, 2003.